A VILLA IN FRANCE

A VILLA IN FRANCE

A novel

by

J. I. M. STEWART

W. W. NORTON & COMPANY

NEW YORK   LONDON

ISBN 0-393-01646-3

Printed in Great Britain

Part One

I

'OUR FRIEND RICH,' the Archdeacon of Oxford had been known to say, 'is inclined to view his sacerdotal function through somewhat antique spectacles. He might come straight out of *Mansfield Park*.' Both these assertions were true, although the second stood in some need of qualification. Henry Rich had taken Holy Orders when the expression 'the family living' could still pass entirely without remark, and it was his expectation that his elder brother, Sir Richard Rich, would in due season present him as a proper person to enter into the enjoyment of just such a benefice. But—as not in the case of Miss Austen's Edmund Bertram—there was some hitch in this convenient arrangement. Henry was not, of course, left out in the cold—there were Rich connections who saw to that—and he suffered no further inconvenience than finding himself, in the year 1933, installed in the vicarage of Mallows in a wholly unexpected part of England. The move brought him, indeed, within reach of his old Oxford college, where he held dining rights of a limited sort; hunting was possible with either the Heythrop or the Old Berks; there proved to be several landowners round about who were benevolently disposed to a parson who was no mean performer with a gun.

Henry was an out-of-doors man and something of an athlete; at Oxford (and this we cannot very readily imagine of Edmund Bertram) he had stroked his college Eight. But he was also quite intelligent after a fashion (it was thus that his tutor spoke of young Rich) and this rendered him occasionally vulnerable to religious doubt. In the main, however, he managed comfortably enough, regarding the priesthood as simply one of the professions open to a gentleman, in which from day to day there is honest work to be done.

When he had been some twelve years at Mallows ill-fortune befell Henry Rich. His wife died, and he was left with their only child, a girl called Penelope, who was scarcely out of her nursery. His physical

7

constitution, which remained exceedingly robust in middle age, for long prompted the expectation that he would marry again, if only for the simplest of carnal reasons. But no such marriage took place. He had been devoted to his wife, and although sexual deprivation was disagreeable it somehow didn't occur to him not to accept it. Being pestered in the matter by several ladies on either their own or a friend's behalf, he even made some changes in his clerical attire suggesting the sort of Anglican High Churchiness that flirts with the doctrine and discipline of clerical celibacy. There was an incongruity about this fox-hunting parson in a soutane that many did not fail to remark. It increased a certain distrust of the vicar which, although seldom spoken aloud, was perceptible among a number of his parishioners. But the older cottagers liked him, saying that he reminded them of Squire Winton, who had owned Mallows Hall before it was bought by the Ferneydales.

'Papa,' Penelope Rich asked over the breakfast table one morning early in her ninth year, 'are the Ferneydales good people?'

Here might have been supposed a question very proper to be propounded by a clergyman's daughter as touching the moral probity of near neighbours. But it was not in this sense that it had been put—a fact indicative of a certain oddity in the notions to which Penelope was being brought up.

'Well, not exactly, my dear,' Mr Rich said amiably. (He was commonly a very good-natured man.) 'They have been respectable people, I don't doubt, for quite a long time. But in a somewhat humble station.'

'A station?' Penelope repeated, puzzled. The word suggested a distant and glamorous region to her, since the nearest railway line was four miles off. On a quiet day, and when the wind was right, you could sometimes faintly hear, romantic as the horns blowing in a tale of chivalry, the long drawn out wail of a steam locomotive.

'Mr Ferneydale's father,' Mr Rich continued, 'was, I believe, an officer in the Indian Army.'

This seemed romantic too, but was evidently designed as not to be received in a wholly favourable light.

'But, Papa'—Penelope spoke as if concerned to vindicate the importance of the Ferneydales—'they live in a very big house.'

'It is certainly bigger than the vicarage.' Watching his daughter finish her porridge, and helping himself to marmalade, Mr Rich laughed easily at this comical conversation. 'Mr Ferneydale is in business. He is what is called a business man. Business men are concerned to make money, as people like ourselves are not. And Mr Ferneydale, I suppose, has succeeded at it rather well.'

Mr Rich was far from speaking as one who held his neighbour and principal parishioner in disregard. The Ferneydales were rich (or so it was believed) and the Riches were poor. But it was the Riches who were, beyond cavil, good people, and a knowledge of this was an element in the perfect complacency with which the vicar regarded the family at the Hall. There was nothing wrong with their manners. The men had been at decent public schools. They did their duty—or at least the parents did—by the parish. James Ferneydale himself even read the lessons on Sunday morning from time to time. It was true that the fellow was rather far from professing himself a believer. But Henry Rich couldn't quarrel with him here, since he had become a little shaky about the Thirty-Nine Articles a good many years back.

'I like Fulke and Caspar Ferneydale,' Penelope said decidedly.

'They appear to be very nice boys—or, rather, young men now.' The vicar had sometimes wondered how the Ferneydales had come to give their two sons those Christian names. 'Their father has told me that there is less than a year between them.'

'So that they just missed being twins?'

'Hardly that.' Mr Rich realized that the facts of life would have to be communicated to Penelope quite soon by one means or another. 'And they are very far from being like twins; from resembling each other, that is, in any way.'

'I like watching them play tennis. I think I understand the rules now, and the funny way of scoring. I'm going to play tennis in my first term at school. And then they'll let me play with them sometimes, perhaps.'

'Do you know, I have enjoyed occasionally watching Fulke and Caspar on the tennis court too?' The vicar's voice had changed slightly. There was nobody much in the parish with whom to talk except in the most discouragingly banal fashion. And already, without being clearly aware of it, he was coming from time to time to treat his daughter as an intelligent grown-up. 'If you know the game fairly well—as I think I do—you see something that bears out what I'm saying: that the brothers are very unlike each other. Fulke's play is imaginative, at times almost freakish—whereas Caspar's is logical. Fulke brings off something that surprises himself; Caspar thinks out a rally as it goes along.'

'What does that mean about which of them is best, and likely to win prizes?' On these occasions Penelope could herself usually manage a bit of a rally; she felt that when her father became interesting like this it was up to her to try hard.

'That's a difficult question. Success in games doesn't depend entirely on the choice and mastery of one or another technique. There's the factor of who most wants to win. Which of these brothers is most a games-player at heart? I think it may be Fulke.'

'You mean Fulke is more determined?'

'Perhaps more determined about some things, and less determined about others. They're both said to be clever. But Caspar is possibly something of an intellectual: a highbrow, as the Americans say. Not powerfully so, perhaps. But the inclination is there.'

Penelope was now out of her depth. But she understood that an analytical comparison was still in progress.

'Mrs Gibbins,' she said, 'has told me Fulke used to do funny things when he was younger.' Mrs Gibbins was the cook. 'But not as young as me.'

Mr Rich didn't respond to this information. He disapproved of gossiping with servants. Instead, he reflected that Penelope, being indeed quite young, was likely to prove a heavy and sometimes perplexing responsibility for many years ahead. He even wondered whether it had been part of his duty to make that second marriage, thereby providing her with such sustained guidance and support as a stepmother might afford. But that, as we have seen, hadn't happened, and he felt it to be too late now. Vaguely in his mind had been the thought that it would do honour to his wife's memory so to contrive matters that their child would one day be mistress in the house from which her mother had been so untimely taken away. But equally—he told himself in a momentary dejection—some sort of selfishness had been at work. He had entrenched himself anew in bachelor habits, and sunk surprisingly deep in them. In none but the most privy relations of life could he imagine the arrival of a strange woman in his household as other than a discommodity and vexation. So he had worked out Penelope's immediate future in terms of governesses and a boarding-school. Mrs Gibbins, a most respectable woman, had been given some extra money and the style of housekeeper. Fortunately she already bore unquestioned authority over the two other maidservants in the vicarage.

'Before you can give the Ferneydales a game,' Mr Rich said, 'you will have to play a good deal of tennis at school, my dear. And perhaps at home too.'

'At home, Papa?'

'It has been in my mind that we ought to have a tennis court. That we are without one is almost an unsuitable thing. Perhaps it might be a hard court, since they are said to be so satisfactory nowadays.'

'That would be very nice,' Penelope said—composedly, although she was round-eyed. She already understood, indeed, that the poverty of the Riches was of a comparative order. Her father kept two hunters—and without any possibility of pretending that they were 'dual purpose' horses. She herself had a pony while several of her friends had to put up with bicycles. But that a tennis court might suddenly appear at the vicarage struck her as very wonderful indeed.

'But, Papa,' she asked virtuously, 'are you sure we can afford it?'

'With some tightening of the belt elsewhere, my dear.' Mr Rich, who was far from being a slim-waisted man, patted himself humorously on the stomach. 'I myself would like to play a little more than I am able to do at present. At my age, you know, a man oughtn't to let himself get too heavy for the saddle.' The vicar said this with the robust conviction he was accustomed to employ when addressing similar admonitions on the Christian life to his humbler parishioners. 'Everybody has a duty to keep fit.'

'Yes, Papa.'

'And now let us think of another duty, Penelope. Are you properly prepared for Mrs Martin today?' Mrs Martin was the current governess, and designed as being the last. She was a vigorous woman who arrived on foot from a neighbouring hamlet every morning, rain or shine, at nine o'clock.

'Yes, I think so. Except that I still have some sentences to translate into French.'

'Then go along and see what you can do about them.'

Being at this time a well-conducted child, Penelope Rich did as she was told and withdrew to the schoolroom, leaving her father to consider more fully the project to which he had more or less committed himself. It was true that he would himself enjoy being able to play tennis other than at the invitation of friends, which was how the matter stood at present. The importance of 'keeping his form' (and he didn't mean in the pulpit) was very real to him. His own father had failed in this regard, turned flabby, and taken to the bottle: a course of things which would be even more censurable in a clergyman than a baronet. His brother Richard, the present holder of the title, was certainly not going to go that way. Richard was an abstinent character—except, indeed, in bed, where he had begotten no fewer than five sons, thereby ensuring that nothing short of unspeakable catastrophe would do anything much for their uncle. Richard was set to become an octogenarian—or a nonagenarian, for that matter—only the more assuredly because he didn't hunt and had therefore almost no chance of breaking his neck. Henry bore no conscious wish to survive his elder brother, and would not have done so even had he been that brother's heir. But he did feel it would be agreeable to wear as well, even in such a trivial matter as continuing to play tolerable tennis at sixty.

Nevertheless it was Penelope he was genuinely considering. As she grew older it would be increasingly important that her home should be attractive to her friends; in particular to suitable schoolfellows when she got round to inviting them to come and stay at the vicarage during holidays. Not all children were taught to ride nowadays. There were people of very good family so wretchedly circumstanced that they simply couldn't find the money for it. But most children played tennis. So a tennis court would be just the right thing, and the cost of its upkeep would be considerably less than that of maintaining the ability to mount three or four young people at a time.

Having finished his breakfast (and after retiring, with a healthy brevity, into what his mother had called private life), Mr Rich went to his study to attend to his correspondence. It was seldom an invigorating task, and the room itself had always struck him as the most depressing in the whole commodiously ugly Victorian house. Architects of that period had felt that clergymen, although entitled to materials and workmanship of the first quality, ought to be so equipped as to afford their peculiar position in society visible embodiment, tangible authentication, in whatever direction they looked or moved. This held especially of an apartment in which sermons were to be composed and godly thoughts entertained. The windows of Mr Rich's study were of gothic configuration and embellished with blobs and rims of coloured glass; the woodwork was of a vestry-like pitch pine; on the encaustic tiles constituting the floor there were to be distinguished designs of half-hearted and non-romish liturgical suggestion; the two doors swung on massive and ramifying wrought-iron hinges, as if they gave not on a breakfast-room and a lobby respectively, but on some superior line in mediaeval tombs. Mr Rich seldom got through his parochial chores amid these surroundings without some fleeting thought of the elegant Georgian rectory of which he had been cheated through that hitch in the matter of the family living. On this occasion he licked his last postage-stamp with satisfaction and made for the open air.

The garden at least was to his taste; reflected his taste, indeed, since he had taken a good deal of care with it. It was under control without being in a suburban fashion tidy and trim, as if here nature could be trusted on a loose rein. Sometimes, when the Old Berks drew the nearer coverts, the pack would come yelping and lolloping across the lawns and even through the flower-beds, while the field waited, strategically poised here and there on the open land beyond. And the damage would be only so much as one could chuckle over or moderately swear about at the end of the day's last run.

Bounding the garden to the south was a stream, and beyond the stream lay the glebe. But just short of this was a flat expanse of turf supposed to have been at one time a bowling green, but now for long resigned to the obscure activities of moles. Mr Rich had been assured that this area was sufficiently elevated above the water, and sufficiently susceptible of enlargement, to admit of the construction of a tennis court on its site. For some minutes he paced up and down in verification of this—moving briskly, since it was a February day of bright sunshine and hard frost. The sun was important; one had to consider how it would be behaving on those late afternoons in summer when play was most likely to be taking place. And then there were the moles: how were they to be eradicated, or at least humanely moved on? Formerly there had been a professional mole-catcher in the village, but when he died nobody had inherited the job. A great many things had changed during and since the war, and now close ahead was the dip into the second half of the twentieth century. Mr Rich—particularly if a little off-colour—was given to reflecting on the unimaginable touch of time—blunting the lion's paws and burning the long-liv'd phoenix in her blood. He occasionally referred sombrely to these effects (and incomprehensibly to the rural mind) in his sermons.

But unless we believe, with some weird sects, that the Grand Combustion lies just round the corner, we have to plan ahead intelligently, despite the fact that an everlasting stream is busy bearing us all away. Mr Rich himself had the duty in particular of so planning ahead for Penelope. He was conscious that he had not always borne financial considerations sufficiently in mind when endeavouring to do this. His manner of life—apart, perhaps, from those two hunters, which were certainly unexampled among the clergy of the diocese—appeared to him in no way inappropriate to a man in his position who was not wholly without private means. The private means, however, were something of a headache. They had been diminishing steadily, and it was even possible to feel that they might one day evaporate altogether amid the disorders of the times. What if his daughter failed to marry—or, what would almost be worse, married some totally penniless person? It was true that a small income was secured to her under a family trust, but it was no more than might decently stand in for a dowry. It would certainly not support her in single life. If that were to be her fate, she would actually have to earn the better part of her living. In an office, it was to be supposed, and as a typewriter. That a Rich might have to become a typewriter was a dire possibility indeed.

Perhaps because from this corner of the vicarage grounds the roof of Mallows Hall was clearly visible, the vicar found his mind turning again to Fulke and Caspar Ferneydale. He was far from clear as to whether or not he regretted their being respectively ten and nine years older than his daughter. Penelope hadn't yet gone to school; these boys were already liberated from it and in their first year at Oxford. That they had gone up to the university in the same term didn't necessarily mean that Caspar was brighter or more precocious than his elder brother. One boy might hang on at a public school even beyond his nineteenth birthday in order to enjoy coveted power and status as a prefect or the like, while another might want to be quit of the place as quickly as he could. This had perhaps been how it stood with the Ferneydales; it chimed in with the vicar's sense—based on only casual association—of the difference between them. Penelope was clearly in the condition of vastly admiring them both indifferently. But the situation was such that she would never be put to the trouble of significantly preferring one to the other.

In a general way one would like one's child to be of an age with what might be thought of as potentially eligible neighbours. But on the whole Mr Rich was well content that Fulke and Caspar would in all probability be married men before Penelope came out. No doubt acceptable and remunerative careers lay ahead of them, and he had no positive reason to suppose that their characters were other than unexceptionable. Nevertheless his approval of them was accompanied by reservations. They weren't exactly—or not so far as he knew—rebels against the accepted order of things as that order was conceived of by people like himself. But at the same time, if in an indefinable way, they didn't quite fit in.

At this point in his ruminations the vicar left his own property through a small gate giving directly on the park of Mallows Hall. James Ferneydale was very insistent that this territory should be regarded by his neighbours, whether gentle or simple, as available to them to walk abroad in and recreate themselves. He made it known that he would wish even his gardens to be similarly accessible. Nobody treated this second wish as other than a somewhat excessive expression of courtesy, indicative of at least a residual sense of social insecurity. But the park was a different matter, and Mr Rich took a short turn in it on most fine days, since this was agreeable in itself and moreover furthered good informal relations with its owner.

His favourite route was round an artificial expanse of water, just large enough to be known as the lake, which lay in a hollow near the centre of the park. It was stocked with water-fowl of an ornamental sort, and in the summer holidays the Ferneydale boys had been accustomed to make it their bathing place. Circling it now, the vicar recalled how, four or five years before, he had come upon them thus engaged—with a very small Penelope sitting on the bank, clasping a doll and seriously regarding them. Diving, swimming, spread-eagled on the grass, the brothers afforded a pleasant spectacle, and Mr Rich had felt no strong prompting to consider it as marred by the fact that they were entirely naked. The young Ferneydales were in a secluded part of their own property, and moreover, as he happened to know, merely maintaining a convention that obtained in the open air swimming pool at their public school. Had Penelope possessed brothers, he would have been far from insisting that their state of nature should invariably be concealed from her—although he might, somewhat illogically, have entertained doubts about the propriety of nudity exhibited the other way on.

He had felt a certain uneasiness upon that occasion, nevertheless. Fulke and Caspar were already far from being small boys. They were tall youths, with the signs of their adolescence apparent upon them. And anybody—some neighbour's maidservant, say, straying aside a little when on an errand to the Hall—might come upon this spectacle unawares. What would the young Ferneydales do then? Would they dive headlong and remain submerged to the chin until the indecorous moment passed, or would they continue capering and showing off? Even as it was, ought they not perhaps to have responded a little more sensitively to the appearance on the bank of a gazing small girl? Mr Rich had known perfectly well that these questions were silly, and he even accused himself of bearing in the matter something very like a prurient mind. But they did betray the fact that in some obscure fashion he slightly distrusted Fulke and Caspar Ferneydale. Later he was to ask himself more than once whether Penelope's continued lively interest in the young males at the Hall had its origin in an incident which, probably enough, was no longer within her conscious memory.

Having rounded the deserted lake on the present occasion, Mr Rich returned home without lingering. The air was chilly still, and more-over it was the day of the week upon which he commonly took a cup of mid-morning coffee with Mrs Martin, and perhaps received from her some account of Penelope's progress. Mrs Martin would not have gone down at all well as any sort of dependant at Mansfield Park; quite as much as Henry Rich she had been brought up on horseback; and although now the impoverished widow of an unsuccessful barrister she had no notion that a governess's place in society is of a lowly and inconsiderable sort. Mr Rich (who shared a good many ideas with Sir Thomas Bertram) had been a little put off by her at first, but had taken to her as soon as he discovered that she got on with her pupil particularly well. Lately he had felt bound to acknowledge that it was sometimes from Mrs Martin that he learnt things about Penelope which, had he been a more talented parent, he would have found out for himself. He was even coming to regret the fact that with the child booked to go off to boarding-school so soon the connection with Mrs Martin must be terminated. Might it not be better that his daughter should continue to be educated at home in the old-fashioned way? Mrs Martin appeared to have a good command of French and German, and he himself could manage Latin and—if such erudition seemed desirable—a little New Testament Greek. There was something pleasant and edifying in the thought of taking Penelope through one of the Gospels in that way.

So over the coffee-cups in the schoolroom, and with the child despatched to attend to her pony, Mr Rich made a cautious approach to these possibilities. Mrs Martin had never evinced any design to set her cap at him, but he had become habitually on his guard against embarrassing misapprehension where eligible ladies were concerned. It would be very dreadful if he appeared merely to be seeking a pretext for securing the governess's continued presence at the vicarage. As it was, Mrs Martin listened to him patiently, and then gave short shrift to his observations.

'There is little to be said, Mr Rich, for preparing a child to live in the manner of its grandparents. Penelope will have to make her way in totally different circumstances.'

'Surely it is young men, Mrs Martin, who have to "make their way" in that sense? When a girl marries——'

'Not all girls marry.'

'That, of course, is true.' Mr Rich had to admit to himself that the possibility of this misfortune befalling his daughter had lately been in his own head.

'Many girls brought up in households like your own are obliged to earn their living, and some are determined to do so, whether they have to or not. Your daughter may turn out to be in one or other of these categories—which may indeed be called the coming thing. And she would be handicapped if she had been denied the companionship, and the stimulus and spirit of emulation and competition, fostered in a good school. Again, she may well want to go to one of the universities.'

'Good heavens!' The vicar was at once intrigued and alarmed by this conjecture. 'You don't mean she's going to be an intellectual?'

'At least she is going to have a clear head. As for Oxford or Cambridge, a girl almost as much as a boy is at a disadvantage if simply privately coached or crammed for entrance to a college.' Having thus spoken with severity, Mrs Martin felt it judicious to let Mr Rich a little off the hook. 'I consider that your existing proposals for Penelope are thoroughly sound.'

'I am glad to hear that. I value your opinion highly, as you must be aware.' The vicar actually contrived a small formal bow over his cup and saucer as he said this—rather with the effect of an eighteenth-century gentleman 'taking wine' with a meritorious fellow-diner. 'But I have a further point in mind. Even at good schools now I gather that one is likely to find a very mixed crowd. For a boy it may be neither here nor there. Indeed, the minor public schools, Rugby and Radley and Repton and Rossall and such places—what one may call the *littera canina* crowd—were developed largely as melting-pots.' Mr Rich paused for a moment, perhaps to allow Mrs Martin to catch up with his small learned joke about the doggy letter. 'They gave the right cast of mind, you know, to the sons of newly prosperous persons. But it is rather different, surely, in the case of a girl. If she makes school-friends outside her own sort of people, undesirable consequences may obviously follow. Their brothers may turn up. That sort of thing.'

'Certainly brothers have everywhere the habit of turning up.' Mrs Martin briefly paused on this, glancing at Mr Rich much in the manner of a naturalist considering whether some small fossilized creature merits preservation under glass. 'You wouldn't care for the idea of Penelope marrying outside what you call her own sort of people?'

'Decidedly not. And surely you agree with me?

'I have some reason for not doing so, Mr Rich. My father, as you may possibly have heard, was a respectable figure in the county: its Lord Lieutenant, in fact. My husband's father was an engine-driver.

Neither Jack nor I found the fact of a discrepant parenthood either here or there.'

'How very interesting!' The vicar uttered this exclamation only in the most feeble fashion. He was appalled at the enormity of his faux pas. It was the more unforgivable in that he could now dimly recall having heard some account of Mrs Martin's distressing history. Charitably, he reflected that with such a *mésalliance* behind her she had done remarkably well.

'I don't know that I'd call it particularly interesting,' Mrs Martin said. 'But it has appealed to Penelope.'

'To Penelope!' The vicar was startled. Indeed, he gave an actual small jump, as he might have done at the appearance of a mouse in his pulpit. 'You have told Penelope the—um—story of your marriage?'

'Dear me, yes. We have had several conversations about marriage, and husbands and wives, and how babies arrive, and that sort of thing.'

Mr Rich almost said 'How very interesting!' again. It was disconcerting thus to discover that Mrs Martin took so broad a view of her pedagogic function, and that had he himself got round to the facts of life with his daughter in the manner he had recently been envisaging, it would have been to find that this somewhat commanding lady had been there before him. He might even have embarked on the subject, been tempted to soften one or two of its odder aspects, and suffered correction by a Penelope who knew just what went where. The thought of this grossness rendering him in fact speechless, he simply waited for what more Mrs Martin had to say.

'Penelope happens to have a romantic view of engine-drivers, and when I told her about Jack's father I went up in her estimation at once. I was reminded of a cousin of mine who took jobs as a private tutor in Vienna between the wars. Several of his pupils were utterly insufferable until he happened to tell them that he knew Edgar Wallace. It was a slight exaggeration, since he'd merely watched the great writer drink a bottle of whisky while holding forth to some undergraduate society. But he declared himself to have been *persönlich bekannt* to this greatest of living Englishmen, and he was regarded with positive awe from then on.'

'I hope Penelope was not insufferable until enlightened about your father-in-law, dear lady.' The vicar found himself saying this with so much recovered good humour and courtly aplomb that he realized anew that he and Mrs Martin got on very well together. Her employment was humble, but she was out of the right stable and you knew where you were with her.

'Penelope was delightful from the start: impetuous at times, but quick to acknowledge a mistake once she became aware of it as that. And I can at least assure you that she doesn't intend to marry into engine-driving circles. She has quite other ideas.'

'God bless my soul! The child loses no time in looking ahead. To an MFH, perhaps? Or a tennis champion or a polar explorer?'

'Penelope intends to marry a poet.'

'A poet!'

'Or a deep philosopher. I think she has quite a lively idea of what a poet is. And there is a deep philosopher in one of her comic picture-books. He sits in a room full of enormous tomes, and is alone except for a cat. I don't feel we need be disturbed over the deep philosopher. But the poet, of course, is another matter. I think he will probably be rather like Shelley.'

Mr Rich saw that he was being made gentle fun of. It seemed to him that—in a harmless way—it was unfairly. He would have acknow-ledged that he was a man of somewhat conventional mind, and that he had just exhibited a commonplace view of what might be in a young girl's head. But it wasn't true that he would prefer a polar explorer to a poet, or even a tennis champion to a deep philosopher, in the character of a son-in-law. He read a little poetry every day, and also believed that if he ever committed anything to the press it would be an unassuming treatise of a philosophical nature—for wasn't he, after all, much interested in that most intractable of metaphysical conun-drums, the Problem of Time?

'What you are really telling me,' he said, 'is something that a parent is no doubt prone to forget, and so I am grateful. A daughter, like a son, has a mind of her own, and a right to such a mind. To oppose any rationally defensible inclination to which it may come is a step to be taken only after the most anxious thought. I invariably make the point when, as sometimes happens, I am consulted in such a situation by parishioners. And I hope I'd stick to it myself. Were Penelope indeed resolved at some future time to go up to one of the ladies' colleges at

Oxford I don't doubt that I should eventually concur in the plan— although I might endeavour to recommend Cambridge, where the women have pitched their camps not quite so close to the men. But marriage is a little different.'

'It is a different branch of education, I suppose.'

'Quite so.' Mr Rich had been uncertain whether this remark was intended as a witticism. There had been an educational aspect to his own marriage, but he had thought of it as consisting in schooling his wife in the consequence of the Riches and the sound conservative views proper to be held in the household of a beneficed clergyman of the Church of England. 'I must confess again,' he now said, 'that I should be unhappy were Penelope to marry other than into our settled and traditional country society.'

'But there is little left either settled or traditional about it, Mr Rich—at least if by "country" you mean "county", as you almost certainly do.' Mrs Martin, a sensible woman but not without her hobbyhorses, seemed suddenly to have decided there were things the Vicar of Mallows ought to hear. 'My father talked about the "county" without the slightest self-consciousness. But now it's a word like "gentleman"—which is what you are when you enter a public lavatory. There's a Cambridge don—male, you'll be glad to know— at Trinity, who.has coined the phrase "the gentry of aspiration". They go back quite a long way, of course. Both Nimrod and Surtees knew them on your hunting-field. But now there are far more of them than there are of your relations, or mine. They are probably the people who are tough enough to take England through what is coming to us. But I suppose we have our prejudices, all the same. Some of them say "the county" so that you curl your toes.'

'That is perfectly true.' The vicar was astonished by the cogency of this remark. It was as if he had gone through life hitherto supposing that toe-curling was a discomfort peculiar to himself alone.

'Have you ever reckoned how many country houses—"country houses" in the old sense—within visiting distance of Mallows are owned by the same families as a hundred years ago? For that matter, do you know how many, throughout England, were simply de- molished last year? Five every week.'

'Gracious lady, spare me!' Mr Rich had taken refuge in a whimsical dismay. *'Tempus ferox, tempus edax rerum.'*

'Time has certainly gobbled up the squirarchy, and it will be the turn of their betters next.'

'Their betters?' The vicar was amazed.

'The great houses are tumbling after the big ones, are they not? Or they're at least what's called "opening up" as show places at half-a-crown a head. I expect your neighbours the Ferneydales may be doing it soon. Although perhaps the Hall is not quite grand enough.'

'No Ferneydales by Reynolds or Gainsborough, eh? An odd name, isn't it? Never heard of it, until those folk arrived in the neighbourhood.'

'It holds at least a pleasingly rural suggestion. And I believe some such name to have been borne by a well-reputed musician.'

'Is that so?' The vicar's tone conveyed both a proper respect for the arts and an underlying sense that a fiddler or the like might be called anything. 'But what we are talking about does constitute a most disturbing trend, of course. Knocking down decent houses, and so forth.' Mr Rich glanced rather misdoubtfully at Mrs Martin, whose tone struck him as lacking the elegiac quality proper to the topic on which they had embarked. He supposed that he was again being made fun of in a fashion. 'As for James Ferneydale, he's a fellow in some big commercial way, and can't stand in need of taking pennies at the door. But it certainly couldn't be said that his family's connection with Mallows is lost in the mists of antiquity.' Mr Rich laughed his secure and good-humoured laugh. 'Any more than mine is—eh, Mrs Martin? Not that one can be sure that money of that sort—the stock market and so on—will still be found tomorrow where it is today. I was thinking about the younger Ferneydales earlier this morning, as a matter of fact, when I was taking my usual turn in the park. Penelope is something of an admirer of the young men. But of course they are too old for her. For dances, and so on. As "escorts", as people say nowadays. I doubt whether they are much aware of her existence— any more, I'm sorry to say, than they are of mine.'

'But if they continue much at home, they may improve their acquaintance, if not with you, yet with Penelope in all sorts of ways.' Mrs Martin's amusement at the direction in which the vicar's mind was moving was not completely masked. 'And what is ten years, after all? You might return from an afternoon's pastoral care—or even an afternoon's fishing—and find that either Fulke or Caspar had carried your daughter off to Gretna Green.'

'Now you want to make my flesh creep.' Mr Rich said this indulgently, but in a tone which at the same time hinted that here was enough of levity. And Mrs Martin, if with a mild irony, at once became more circumspect.

'But I don't know that they *will* continue much at home,' she said. 'They don't often turn up at people's parties, but I run into them from time to time, and I'm always pleased when it happens. There's a certain liveliness in their talk, which I imagine is already standing them in good stead at Oxford. It's something we are a little short of in these parts.'

'It is, indeed, Mrs Martin—and one of the reasons why *I* so much enjoy running into *you*.' This sort of compliment was something that the vicar knew how to carry off very well. 'Do the young Ferneydales complain about us as a dull crowd at Mallows?'

'It may be what they say to one another, but they don't to me, any more than they would to you. There's nothing boorish about them. All they do is to express themselves as a little baffled by those who find steady satisfaction in country pursuits.'

'They certainly don't hunt.'

'No, indeed. Fulke says he doesn't like horses, and Caspar declares that he finds Jeremy Bentham's condemnation of killing foxes for sport to be unanswerable, and that he can't understand how a man who would feel insulted by an invitation to go cock-fighting or bull-baiting is content to make a far greater nuisance of himself hallooing over the countryside, pursuing one quadruped while be-striding a second and urging on a whole rabble of howling and snuffling others.'

'One has to acknowledge that very generous feelings may be enlisted in the case against fox-hunting.' Mr Rich said this stoutly and honestly at once—while at the same time telling himself how right was his instinct a little to distrust the young men at the Hall. 'But I wish I knew them rather better,' he went on conscientiously. 'They do at least sound stimulating. Do you know much about their more positive interests?'

'Caspar, I think, is inclined to be studious.'

'Ah, yes! I believe I'd have guessed that. Walks about with a book under his arm.' Mr Rich, being by profession a clerk and man of learning, naturally didn't say this in a disparaging way. But he didn't sound exactly approbatory, either.

'So he does. And he much wants to be up to date. So the book is probably by Kierkegaard.'

'Kierkegaard?' The vicar was puzzled. 'Kierkegaard was some sort of gloomy Dane. Like Hamlet, you might say, seeing everything out of joint at Elsinore. But he must have died more than a hundred years ago. He can't even be as up to date as the old bore Ibsen.'

'He may have returned into vogue. Indeed, I have gathered so much from Caspar himself. Caspar tells me that he has clarified his speculative position and finds himself to be an Existentialist.'

'Finds himself a fiddlestick! He's a schoolboy—or was, the day before yesterday. And we're all for existing, I suppose: foxes and fox-hunters and natterers about cruel blood-sports.' Mr Rich, who had begun this speech in his most tolerant tone, seemed to regret its having gone astray. 'But Fulke,' he went on quickly, '—what about him?'

'Fulke is a very observing young man. I have even teased him as being just like a private eye.'

'Like a what?' The vicar was at a loss before this strange expression.

'A kind of up-dated Sherlock Holmes, with a very pale-blue and penetrating gaze. I am rather inclined to respect it in Fulke Ferneydale. He seems to me to possess real intellectual curiosity. Of course he expresses it in a half-baked way. I asked him once what he intended to do when he left Oxford, and he told me that he was going to be an experimental psychologist.'

'And just what is that, Mrs Martin?'

'I asked him that too. He said it is one who subjects a human guinea-pig to excessive bewilderments and notes the precise length of time that these take to drive the unfortunate individual mad.'

'I don't think I like the sound of Fulke.'

'He may be better than he sounds. Remember that he is only a nineteen-year-old boy, conscious of ability and bored with his home surroundings—and that he was being badgered by an elderly female who goes about teaching children their ABC.'

'I can't see you badgering anybody, Mrs Martin. But you do appear to be quite interested in this young man.' Mr Rich made his remark sound ever so slightly comical. Stopping just short of face-tiousness was part of the technique of what Mrs Martin called his pastoral care.

'It would be very tiresome to him if it were apparently so. Perhaps I am just a little bored myself. But I hope that at least I don't seem vulgarly inquisitive when I have the chance of casual talk with Fulke Ferneydale. For I do feel that he is a young man with a secret.'

'Dear me!' The vicar disapproved, if not of a young man having a secret, at least of his revealing the fact to a lady. 'Does Fulke go out of his way to suggest himself as intriguingly mysterious?'

'Nothing of the sort. It is a wholly involuntary betrayal. Or you may say I simply divine that he knows something about himself—perhaps something about a bent or capacity—which Mallows would find perplexing. But I don't think it's anything sinister. He certainly doesn't give the impression of being without a good deal of confidence about himself. He is an ambitious youth.'

'You make me feel remiss, Mrs Martin, in not knowing more about him. Only this morning I was speaking confidently, indeed, to Penelope about how the brothers play tennis. But that is a matter of quite superficial observation, and beyond it I have only a general notion of their differing temperaments. The truth is I feel a little diffident about the young Ferneydales, since I can scarcely claim them as belonging to my flock. Neither of them has so much as come to matins of a Sunday for many months. It may be sloth—in itself not a trivial weakness. But I sadly fear they see themselves positively as highly enlightened infidels.'

'I don't know about Fulke. Caspar has recently been received into the Roman Catholic Church.'

'Good heavens!' The vicar had sprung to his feet in great agitation. 'The boy might at least have let me know. My predecessor christened him, and he was confirmed at his school in the normal and proper way. It's a most uncivil thing.'

'That is one aspect of it, no doubt.'

'I have always thought of Caspar Ferneydale as at least decently brought up. How can he have decided to flout me in so grave a case?'

Mrs Martin might have said, 'He disapproves of your hunting', or even, 'He laughs at your going about in *les jupes*'. But she had been needlessly upsetting, and regretted it. So she held her peace.

'You don't think that Fulke's precious secret may simply be that he has become a Hindu?' The vicar achieved this sarcasm only with an effort. 'And the boy's father!' he burst out again. 'He ought surely to have alerted me. It's a serious matter—perversion to papistry in a household of some standing in the neighbourhood. I'd never have supposed James Ferneydale capable of being so neglectful of a duty. It will be my own duty to make my displeasure known to him.'

'If you feel you must tackle somebody, ought it not to be Caspar in person?' Mrs Martin, who liked Mr Rich and didn't care to think of him doing something foolish, was unconcerned at any failure to comport herself as a governess should. 'And in a spirit of friendly enquiry, really. I gather there are Catholic Existentialists, but it nevertheless sounds a little heterodox. You might ask Caspar to explain that particular position. Positions are rather his thing. He is still very young in all his ways, of course, but he has a restless intelligence which promises I don't know what. He might enjoy informed conversation with you. I doubt whether either his brother or his father is much interested in theological questions. And although I'm inclined to think that Fulke has the most interesting character in the family I'm fairly confident that Caspar has the most interesting mind.'

During these composing remarks the vicar had taken a turn up and down his daughter's schoolroom. And when he came to a halt before his daughter's governess it was to an unexpected effect.

'Dear lady,' he said, 'you may well be right. I give weight to your words, as I should always wish to do, and it may be that I would indeed be wrong were I to make a personal matter of this. We live, after all, in an ecumenical age. We must remember that an eirenic spirit is abroad, and that in its light the Christian Church is to be seen as essentially one and indivisible. Caspar Ferneydale may cure himself of his vagary, and if he is as intellectual as you appear to believe he will arrive all the more quickly at a perception of the errors of Rome.'

Mr Rich (who believed strongly in comfortable states of mind) had arrived at this more accommodating view of things with surprising speed, and certainly without any sense of involving his argument in contradiction. Mrs Martin might have congratulated herself on handling the situation with considerable address. But in fact as she

26

walked home at the end of the day's lessons it was in a self-critical mood.

On the question of Penelope's future education, indeed, she had managed well enough. No more would be heard of the child's continuing to be taught at home. From Mrs Martin's own point of view this was to be regretted, since she was fond both of Penelope and of the vicar's monthly cheque. If Henry Rich was something of a goose (and she did so regard him in a perfectly friendly way) he might be said—although sexually the metaphor was slightly confused—to lay agreeable little golden eggs. But Mrs Martin, being a woman of spirit, had no difficulty in disregarding this. She judged that a girl brought up entirely in the Mallows vicarage under its present incumbent, although she might know about *tempus ferox* and the doggy letter, would eventually have to step ill-prepared into the contemporary world from a dwelling as remote, it might be said, as Noah's Ark. Penelope Rich was a child for whom the right boarding-school would be very much the right thing.

But about the Ferneydale boys Mrs Martin hadn't done so well. She had enhanced in the vicar a distrust of them which she knew to be already there, and this on the strength of mere coffee-time conversation thoughtlessly carried on. She didn't share Mr Rich's view that Fulke and Caspar were 'too old' for Penelope. All that could confidently be said was that at present she was too young for them. The situation—as, indeed, she had pointed out to the vicar—might be quite different ten years on. So it had been injudicious to prejudice a conceivable state of affairs in which Penelope was of marriageable age and still possessed as close neighbours at Mallows Hall two able and attractive young bachelors whom she had vastly admired as a child.

Mrs Martin held no view on the general desirability or undesirability of matrimony succeeding upon long contiguity of that sort. It was a species of conduct popularly regarded as a resource which young men held in reserve while hoping for some more glamorous fortune, and she didn't like to imagine Penelope as being thus fallen back upon by a Ferneydale. It was, of course, a far-fetched apprehension. Not quite so far-fetched was the fear that Penelope mightn't marry at all. Nothing of the kind was at present her father's wish; he had spoken only of anxiety that his child should make a right choice in the end. But Henry Rich was both a widower and a self-regarding if well-meaning man. Mrs Martin could think of more than one daughter of a widowed clergyman permanently entombed in the paternal vicarage or rectory in a strikingly grisly way—having been progressively pressurized into the belief that neither her parent nor his parish could do without her. The risk of this fate befalling Penelope Rich might be lessened at some critical time if she had behind her a girlhood spent largely away from home.

Having arrived at this perception, Mrs Martin felt that her firmness about her pupil's future schooling had been doubly wise.

II

'OH, SEX!' FULKE Ferneydale said. 'I can tell you about sex, Cass. Sex is all balls.'

Fulke and his brother were at this time in their second term at Christ Church and New College respectively. When a choice fell to be made (for they were both academically promising enough to have a say in the matter) they had agreed that they didn't want to be in the same dump at Oxford, having had enough of that at school. So they picked out two colleges they both thought they could tolerate, tossed up between them, and filled in statements of preference accordingly. But it had turned out that they were now seeing more of one another than before. Both were quite sociable in a general way, and each was in process of forming a circle of acquaintance largely unknown to the other. But the university was still full of men coming back from the war, many of them married, and the first generation of boys arriving again directly from school was rather shy of these mature persons, so that the customary undergraduate process of rapidly acquiring intimate friends was constricted as a result. It was only to a small extent because of this, however, that the Ferneydales had formed the habit of meeting once or twice a week and talking much as young men do when thrown together amid assumptions of adulthood for the first time. Both felt—though without precisely articulating the idea—that they had hitherto taken one another for granted in a childish and unenterprising way, and that they were now developing, as their interests broadened, a kind of reciprocal intellectual curiosity which had been largely foreign to their habit at home. Caspar (whom we have heard of as liking to clarify positions) had put part of the situation into forthright words. 'We're really trying,' he had said, 'to decide whether we particularly like one another. Siblings often don't.'

At the moment, at least, the siblings were getting on quite well. Caspar was drinking Fulke's madeira and Fulke was smoking

Caspar's *Gauloise* cigarettes. They were sitting comfortably on either side of a window embrasure in the rather grand rooms that Fulke had somehow wangled for himself in Peckwater quad. And they had fallen upon a topic that was naturally of interest to them both.

'All balls?' Caspar echoed. 'Nonsense, you mean?'

'Well, in that sense, too. But literally, in the first place. I was offering you an ambiguity, as a matter of fact, and I think it's rather neat. Sexual orientation and behaviour have their variations, as Havelock Ellis so tediously demonstrates. But sex always comes down to balls in the end.'

'Not among Lesbians, I suppose.'

'You're quite coming on, Cass,' Fulke said tolerantly. 'Never an impure thought used to be your line—although I did once or twice hear you called a boot-cupboard type. Don't tell me you're becoming *troubled* about sex? Does it rear its dirty head in the night?'

'Don't be silly. If you want to know, I have regular wet dreams about struggling to get between the legs of naked girls—and extremely indecent and intermittently sadistic reveries or fantasies or whatever they're called, as well.'

'How very shocking!' Fulke, if not really shocked, was genuinely surprised by this frank communication. Hitherto, his brother had been notably buttoned up on such topics as this. He was a theoretical type, Fulke reflected. Perhaps amid much inadequate performance he was going to retreat upon extravagant words. 'How *more* than shocking! And what does your infallible Church say about such goings on?'

'The Church isn't all-round infallible. It's mere ignorance to suppose it claims to be. The Church is pretty awful, as a matter of fact, and always has been. Fortunately, there's the Faith.'

'I see.' This, Fulke realized, must be the modish thing to say among Caspar's Oxford co-religionists. His brother was always anxiously up to date, at least on ideological fronts. 'Well, what does the Faith say about licentious imaginings?'

'It's rather complicated, I believe. I'm going to discuss it with Father Fisher at the Chaplaincy.'

'That should be most stimulating. Have you discussed Existentialism with Father Fisher?'

'Yes, of course. But I'm a little changing my views there. Have you read Camus, Fulke?'

'I've read a novel about a plague at Oran, which came out a couple of years ago. Quite good. At least not all balls.'

'I'm thinking of something rather earlier: an essay called *Le Mythe de Sisyphe*. It sets out his position, and has impressed me very much. I can see Jaspers in it, and perhaps Heidegger too. But I don't think Camus is really an Existentialist. And Monsieur Sartre agrees with me.'

Caspar Ferneydale had shown considerable enterprise in getting twice to post-war Paris, and even more in securing for himself, as a well-conducted and intellectually precocious youth, the occasional *entrée* to certain quite imposing literary gatherings. It had thus come about that he had actually been presented to the distinguished writer he had just named. So nowadays, even in familiar conversation, he always said 'Monsieur Sartre' where others would say simply 'Sartre', thus contriving to intimate the existence of a personal acquaint-anceship which he wished, nevertheless, to be understood as judiciously respectful on his part. Fulke was a good deal impressed by his brother's achievement in even precariously making this exalted grade; he owned a shrewd awareness of what is known in sporting circles as 'class'; and he was quick to recognize its evidences both in the writing of fiction (which he found an absorbing subject) and also in various fields he knew comparatively little about. 'My Achilles heel,' he had lately told Caspar, 'is an unwholesome respect for my betters.' Whereupon Caspar had looked surprised—but had then immediately said, 'Yes, that's perfectly true.'

Both the brothers were now on their feet and prowling in an unco-ordinated way about the room, which with its two big windows was large enough to admit of this exercise without danger of collision. Perhaps because as boys they had put in a good deal of time playing fast-moving games together (sometimes to the admiration of the little Penelope Rich), or perhaps for obscurer reasons, each tended to induce a kind of physical restlessness in the other. At the moment, however, Caspar had the motive of inspecting whatever Fulke had recently been adding to his possessions in college. He told himself as he did so that Fulke on a similar quest in New College would be shamelessly rifling drawers and peeping into cupboards, contending that it is by detective work like this that one can best fulfil one's duty to discover as fully as one can just how other people tick. Caspar himself was content to examine books, gramophone records and pictures. The books were becoming numerous and were notably miscellaneous. Many were in French, for there was common ground between the brothers here.

'Why do you never have much poetry on your shelves?' Caspar asked curiously.

'I don't like black marks straggling about a page. My eye bounces off anything that doesn't show a good straight margin right as well as left. It makes me feel the printer hasn't done his job—justifying his type, or whatever it's called.'

'How silly can we get.'

'All right, Cass. Poetry can do nothing that can't be better done in prose. Metre was invented mainly to make remembering easier before Homer and all that crowd had got round to inventing writing. But also because it sends you half-asleep, so that you're the less able to distinguish between sense and nonsense. Think of that awful *Paradise Lost*. Nasty rubbish driven home by the banging of tomtoms in the jungle. But some people like it that way. "Poetry gives most pleasure when none too intelligible." Coleridge or a similar pundit said something like that.'

'Not quite like that. And to my mind poetry is a high-powered engine for exploring reality.'

'How very grand!' Fulke, who had been gazing absently out of a window, turned round and nodded quite soberly. 'Of course I agree that's the general idea of literature: what they call imaginative literature, that's to say. Finding out. But it has to keep to experimental method.'

'Oh, lord! Is this experimental psychology again?'

'Yes, it is. The novelist or the playwright—and nobody else is worth considering—is most definitely an experimental psychologist. He devises and sets up his experiment—such and such a clutch of chaps in such and such a situation—and then observes and records what happens.'

'You can't believe such balderdash, Fulke. Nothing happens that your writer doesn't *make* happen.' Caspar was seriously concerned. 'He has to provide out of his own head all the dynamism required. It's his own intuitive sense of how human character and motive work that he's "recording", as you call it, all the time.'

32

'Well, yes, Cass—but it comes to rather the same thing. The myth of the characters taking charge and di~tating to their creator does have some validity. It simply means that the novelist or whosoever has acquired—and it's a matter of ceaseless observation and experience—what the trick-cyclists call insight. And that he has to obey it. Don't you agree?'

'I think I go quite a long way with you, Fulke. Only I'm not at all sure that the novelist or dramatist gets his characters quite that way. Or not at his most effective that way: by observation and whatever. I think it's rather a matter of his giving an airing to sundry alternative selves. He had elected his own personality, you know, from a whole heap of stuff offering. But he lets others, still stirring in him, have a spin. Herbert Read says——'

'Bugger Herbert Read! He's just another of your idea-mongers.'

'Have you read *The Green Child*?'

'Yes, I have. Alpha in its rum way. But he wrote it in time off from concocting stuff to muddle heads like yours. Get on with saying something for yourself, Cass.'

'Very well. I say the great writer gets his characters not by peering through key-holes, but by a process of projecting upon the page his perhaps unacknowledged selves. It's what Coleridge meant—since you're so fond of quoting him, Fulke—by calling Shakespeare myriad-minded. And Yeats by cribbing from him and talking about many-minded Homer.'

'So Iago can be called one of Shakespeare's unacknowledged selves?'

'Oh, decidedly.'

'And so can Desdemona? We seem to be back with the wily serpent sex. Poor old Shakespeare had a gaggle of wenches bottled up inside him?'

'Of course you can express the thing grotesquely if you want to, Fulke. But at least it's an observed fact that a great many abundantly creative people have been noticeably bisexual. I've been reading an interesting chap who has a good deal to say about that. And he says the incidence is to be remarked not merely in artists of one sort or another, but in geniuses in general. Christ, for example.'

'Heavens above! What does your Father Fisher think of *that* one?'

'We happen not to have discussed the matter.' Caspar had been a little disconcerted by this question. 'At least it's an interesting theory.'

'Interesting tommy-rot.' Fulke had become abruptly impatient. 'Who said "now Master up, now Miss"?'

'Alexander Pope. He makes it rhyme with "vile antithesis"—which is rather intolerant, I think. But he was speaking of a chap who was no sort of artist or genius at all.'

'Isn't it just that everybody is a bit bisexual, at least in a phylogenetic way? You need only bare your manly chest to prove the point, Cass. And no doubt the fact is revealed at times in impulses as well as tits. But it's a completely boring and useless one when you come to talking about literature and art and what-not. The only important thing there is to know what's tiptop, and to go for it.'

'To manage that successfully, you have to be tiptop.' Caspar was now regarding Fulke curiously. He had suspected for a long time where his brother's ambition lay, and now here it seemed to be. 'And that's where one comes to the limiting factor in your theory of the novelist as working from observation and experience. If what he is capable of observing is only the superficial levels of human behaviour, and if his experience is largely bookish and second-hand, then his end result will be conventional and stereotypic. It may be highly amusing and even brilliant in various ways. Aldous Huxley, you know. But genuinely exploratory it simply will not be. Only high art *reveals*—creates knowledge, if you like, as the great scientists do.'

Caspar, who had delivered these pronouncements ruthlessly, and with a confidence perhaps born of his recently acquired French connections, suddenly came to a halt before a picture on the wall. It was a small painting by Modigliani of not at all a small-seeming salmon-pink nude girl. Caspar paused for a moment to make sure it wasn't a colour-print, but indeed an original properly to be confronted with stupefaction.

'Good God!' he then said. 'It's a Modi. How on earth have you come by it?'

'I bought it from a man.' Fulke, whose manner had been rather sombre during the latter part of this colloquy, became amused again. 'Is that what your Parisian friends call him—Modi?'

'It's another ambiguity for you, or at least a pun. *Maudit*. The poor chap was very much that. Fulke, you must have given everything you had in the bank for it.'

34

'Yes, I did.'

'I find it rather a surprise. If you were to become a writer——'
Caspar broke off. 'Or let's come clean. It's what's in your head, and
you're bound to make it. But I'd think of you as working, broadly
speaking, in the tradition of realism. *Madame Bovary* and *Boule de Suif*
and *The Old Wives' Tale*. I'm not quite clear about the appeal to you of
a chap like Modi.'

'Thanks a lot. You don't half put me among the swells.' Fulke was
grinning with an unwonted nervousness. 'But, you see, I like eclectic
skills. Reaching out to this and that and putting something rather
fresh-looking together. But then it has to look, as we were saying,
tiptop.'

'Is that what Modigliani manages?'

'Obviously. Botticelli and Benin sculpture, Tuscany and the Heart
of Darkness. You have to be a swell to manage a synthesis like that.'
Fulke was standing before a window again. 'Would you like to see my
tutor? If so, there he is.'

Such an abrupt change of subject didn't greatly please Caspar, who
felt that he and Fulke had been on the verge of establishing a new
relation of confidence. But he joined his brother at the window. The
view was dominated by an ancient building known formally in the
college as the New Library, and about to round a corner of this was an
elderly man in cap and gown clutching half-a-dozen books.

'Watch!' Fulke said.

What was to be watched was the odd sight of this learned pedes-
trian apparently caught up and driven off-course by a tremendous
gale, which obliged him to pursue a circuitous route quite alien to his
intention.

'Why on earth does he behave like that?' Caspar asked.

'Every day he remembers just in time that a chunk of the library
may come down and flatten him into a pancake. You can see what it's
like: a ruined Greek temple at Paestum or somewhere, but in considerably worse repair than that. It has been crumbling for several
centuries. Dr Johnson mentions it, as a matter of fact, in a poem you
probably know, since you like the stuff. *Here falling houses thunder on your
head.* That's why this college is familiarly known as the House, of
course.'

35

'Is it really dangerous?' Caspar judged it unnecessary to take notice of much of this routine nonsense, familiar to him in Fulke's talk. 'It certainly looks as if it is.'

'Lord, yes! It carried off three of our dons only this winter. But more keep coming forward—which is remarkable, considering the ghastly life they lead. Which must be the more excruciating to have to listen to, I sometimes wonder: the sort of silly-clever essay I concoct weekly, or the abjectly moronic ones turned in by most of the other young gentlemen? I suppose, Cass, you realize you'll have to become a don yourself? Unless, that is, you renounce the papists, take Anglican orders, and succeed that old donkey, Henry Rich. It's the right thing for a younger son.'

'And what about you as an elder one? Do you imagine yourself following a squirarchal life at Mallows?'

'Certainly not. Not even if there's going to be a squirarchal life there to follow—which I begin to doubt. Of course *notre père* keeps his cards damn close to his chest, and I haven't managed to discover anything very positive by poking about.'

'What do you mean—poking about? You've actually been asking people to tell you the state of the business, and so on?'

'Naturally I have—and I've been keeping a look-out for letters lying around, too. Consenting to live in ignorance, you know, is the cardinal intellectual sin. Or so I think. We might have another of our clever little chats about it.'

'You're pretty awful, Fulke. You really are.'

'Perhaps so. But the point is that I suspect there isn't going to be much coming our way. Father is almost certainly living most reprehensibly beyond his means. He's already yattering about my being called to the bar.'

'It seems to me not a bad idea—and I believe a lot of writers have begun that way.' Caspar was uncomfortable before this turn in the conversation. 'Incidentally, who do you think was dining at our High Table last night? Henry Rich himself. And it didn't seem to be as anybody's guest. He struck me as just loose around the place, under his own abundant steam.'

'I suppose he's a New College man—and before that I'd say he'd been what they call a Harrovian of the old school. Didn't he call on you, Cass, and engage in theological disputation?'

'There's no reason to suppose he knows I'm up at New College. But *I* ought to have called on *him*, as a matter of fact. Quite some time ago, I mean, to tell him I was signing off his conventicle. It would have been the civilized thing to do, and I've no wish to offend him. That's quite a decent kid of his, although I expect she's being brought up as a little snob and prig. The trouble with Rich is that it's hard to take him seriously.'

'I've just thought of an experiment with him,' Fulke said, suddenly interested. 'A little like the one with Mrs Whitty, but better.'

'It might easily be that.' Caspar disapproved of his brother's experiments, which he regarded as no more than offensive practical jokes. Mrs Whitty was a widow, and presided over the Mallows post-office and primitive general store. Several years before, Fulke had contrived to circulate in the village a rumour to the effect that Mrs Whitty had come into a substantial inheritance from an American cousin, but was for some perverse reason keeping dark about it. A number of the male inhabitants of Mallows found this intelligence as noteworthy as they were designed to do, and Fulke had particular hopes of Bill Sheen the thatcher, who had seduced a sufficient number of village girls to be presumably ready for any regular union carrying advantageous consequences in the serious concerns of life. Unfortunately very little had come of this in the end, but for weeks Fulke had entertained himself with close observation of what he supposed to be a developing comedy.

'I'd send our man of God——' Fulke began.

'Your man of God.'

'I'd send my man of God a telegram, and manage to be in the post-office when it arrived, so that I could innocently offer to take it up to the vicarage myself. And then I'd observe closely the successive emotional states educed in this muscular Christian by the news.'

'Just what news?'

'The telegram would announce that Rich's brother and all five of his nephews had perished in a marine catastrophe. In other words, it would be the Reverend Sir Henry Rich, Baronet of somewhere-or-other, who stood before me. I'd condole, but also offer my respectful felicitations. One auspicious and one dropping eye, as Shakespeare has it. What do you think of that?'

'A shade lacking in subtlety, perhaps.' For a moment Caspar

37

considered the adequacy of this mildly ironic reply. 'Or rather, just too bloody stupid and oafish for words. And the telegram, I imagine, might take you before the magistrates. If it did, the only question in their minds would be whether you were too old to send to Borstal.'

'Do you know, Cass, I'm afraid all that is perfectly true?' Fulke was not at all offended by this brotherly candour. 'Nevertheless, the theory of the contrived test or confrontation remains an interesting and perfectly valid one. *Hamlet*, again! Think of the play scene.'

'Superb experimental psychology, no doubt. But don't, by the way, try out anything of the sort on me, Fulke. Not if you'd avoid a bloody nose, old boy. But thanks for the drink.'

'Any time,' Fulke Ferneydale said.

Caspar Ferneydale did, in the event, pay a formal call on the Vicar of Mallows. This was much to his credit as a genuinely courteous young man; and the more so since the call awkwardly followed upon a *fait accompli*. Mr Rich, it is true, was unaware that Caspar regarded him as one whom it was hard to take seriously, and who was probably bringing up a daughter as a little snob and prig; nor did anything in Caspar's manner during the visit so much as faintly hint disrespect. But the visit was demonstrably a foray from the achieved citadel of Holy Church, unpreceded by any troubled intimation of doubts as to the validity of the Anglican position, and it was therefore impossible to disguise the fact that nothing more than a social propriety was being observed.

But Mr Rich approved of social proprieties, and moreover he was quickly aware that it was a well-educated as well as well-mannered young man who had turned up in his study. Almost his only habitual visitors were female parishioners who were either obtrusively devout (which was embarrassing) or boringly concerned with Sunday School outings or jumble sales or the embroidering of hassocks which there would eventually be few to kneel on. Caspar appeared more speculatively than devoutly inclined, but he was presumably at least less interested in hassocks than in cassocks; what he had come to speak about, even if a sad error, was not at all trivial but rather to be regarded as of grave import. This in itself was a pleasant change. And Mr Rich, anxious on his part not to appear perfunctory in his reception of what was being communicated to him, ventured some cautious remarks of a theological nature, and even asked Caspar if he had any intention of entering the priesthood. To this the young man made a guarded reply. Nevertheless the conversation continued for some time.

'I happen to have heard from our common friend Mrs Martin,' the vicar said politely, 'that you take a considerable interest in the thought of Sören Kierkegaard.' (The vicar had refreshed his memory of the Danish sage following that conversation.) 'I have been told that he was the original of Ibsen's hero in *Brand*. *Brand* is scarcely, to my mind, among the most successful of Ibsen's plays.' (The vicar produced this with perfect aplomb.) 'But there is certainly a link between the two in an implacable hostility to all institutional religion. So I am surprised that you can build Kierkegaard into—shall we say?—the Roman Catholic pantheon.'

Caspar smiled engagingly by way of receiving this. It would have been impossible to guess that he was vastly amused by Mr Rich's transparent satisfaction in thus sustaining a donnish rather than a clerical rôle. One could be quite certain that the man didn't know the first thing about Kierkegaard. But Kierkegaard was at this time a little fading from Caspar's own mind. Father Fisher at the Chaplaincy had come down against him, and had recommended a study of Maritain. There would be no point, however, in tackling this old donkey on neo-Thomism. So Caspar offered what he knew would sound a baffling remark about Kierkegaard's having been 'trampled to death by geese', and prepared to bring his duty call to an end.

But at this moment there came a knock at the vicar's study door, and it opened to admit Penelope Rich. Caspar Ferneydale took one look at the child—who had recently passed her ninth birthday—and at once got to his feet.

Mr Rich approved of this politeness. Penelope, whether she approved of it or not, produced a more than adequate response in the form of a prompt curtsy: behaviour of a Victorian-nursery order which she was inwardly resolved to have no more of once she had got away to school. But she was pleased with Caspar, all the same. She had come into the room to break the news that the vet had called, and had pronounced Jolly Boy, the vicarage pony, to be suffering from mange. The position was a delicate one, since Miss Hiscock, with whom the vicarage hunters were now kept ('at livery', as Mr Rich liked to express it) at the other end of the village, had positively delivered herself of a contrary opinion. Penelope knew that her father was bound to be upset. And she found the unexpected presence of Caspar Ferneydale disconcerting, since she judged mange to be a disreputable affliction, the presence of which at the vicarage must be to the discredit not only of her father and herself, but also of all Riches throughout the land. So she said nothing, but waited to be addressed.

'My dear, I think you know Mr Caspar Ferneydale?' the vicar said, amiably if with the slight excess of formality habitual in him. 'My daughter,' he then said to Caspar, 'is a great admirer of your tennis.'

This wasn't quite as bad as 'My daughter likes you very much' would have been. Even so, it represented the violation of a confidence, so that Penelope coloured faintly and offered Caspar a smile more distancing than she intended. Her feeling about her father in such matters, if put into words, would have been that he meant kindly but wasn't always reliable.

'Oh, well,' Caspar said modestly, 'I can just give my brother a game. It doesn't amount to more than that.' The kid's having come into the room like this, he told himself, was distinctly useful. His call could now end in a few minutes' time on a purely social and neighbourly note. 'Not that it looks,' he went on, 'as if we'll be having much tennis this season at the Hall. There's been a tremendous invasion by moles.'

'By moles!' The vicar was aghast. The vicarage moles had been persuaded to migrate as his own tennis court got under way. But it looked as if they had done so in a deplorable direction, and were now to be described as (so to speak) at livery with the Ferneydales. In fact it appeared that tennis attracted them just as it did his daughter. 'They have really attacked,' Mr Rich added, 'your father's admirable court?'

'In quite a big way, sir.' This was the first time, on the present occasion, that Caspar had said 'sir' to the vicar. Caspar had a lively period sense, and believed that the lavish employment of the word towards one's seniors had lately been passing from the old to the new gentry, so that it had become a stockbrokerish and commuter-belt sort of thing. But Henry Rich, who belonged pretty well before the

Flood, would certainly regard it as *de rigueur* and wholly 'U' ('U' was a very recent invention) as from a younger to an older man. 'It looks like a bomb-site. And the gardeners don't seem to know what to do about it.'

'You have a step-ladder,' Penelope said suddenly. 'You put it over a molehill, and you wait on it with a shotgun for twelve o'clock.'

'Midnight?' Caspar asked. Penelope, he decided, was much less boring than her father.

'No—the middle of the day. Moles have something like a little watch inside their heads, and at twelve o'clock they move up towards the sun. So at twelve o'clock you fire your gun straight down into the molehill and kill one mole, or perhaps even two.'

'My dear child!' The vicar allowed himself a moment's kindly laughter. 'Wherever did you hear such nonsense?'

'From Mrs Martin, papa. She told me that her father had great faith in it. He would do it every day for weeks. And then the moles would give up and go away. Bearing their dead with them, Mrs Martin says.'

'Like the dolphins, Penelope,' Caspar interposed. 'And with their wounded. They get them away too.'

'Well, well!' If his daughter's information brought Mr Rich a little to a stand it was because he recollected that Mrs Martin's father had been—doubtless among other distinctions—Lord Lieutenant of the county. 'Then your tennis must be played here at the vicarage,' he said, turning to his visitor. (He was coming quite to approve of the absurd young papist.) 'As you may have heard, I am having a hard court constructed now. It will certainly be at the service of your family, my dear Caspar'—this was an astonishing mark of favour—'until your own beautiful turf is in order again.'

'That's most kind of you, sir.' (Caspar thought he might as well be hanged for a sheep as a lamb.) 'I'll look forward to the pleasure of being well licked by you myself.'

'Certainly, certainly—or the other way round.' Mr Rich seemed to find this, although oddly expressed, an entirely agreeable proposal. And a capital idea now occurred to him. He felt that—with the exception of that cryptic bit about Kierkegaard being trampled to death by geese—he had kept his end up fairly well with this bright young man from Oxford. But he wanted no more of it for the moment.

His tennis was a little rusty, but not so rusty as his theology. And, given another go, the boy might bombard him with Teilhard de Chardin—the Chinese monkey-man, he vaguely recalled—and heaven knew what. 'You must really see how our court is coming on,' he said. 'And it would be a kindness to let Penelope show it to you. She's tremendously looking forward to learning to play on it herself—and perhaps against you, one day. That's so, isn't it, my dear?'

'Yes, papa.' Penelope was sufficiently offended to dissimulate her excitement at this idea and to speak in the resigned tone of a dutiful daughter. 'Only if Mr Ferneydale has the time, of course.'

This was not encouraging, and moreover Caspar was unable to feel that much interest could attach to inspecting a half-made tennis court. But the child herself attracted him. So he made his bow to Mr Rich, was benignly shaken hands with, punctiliously opened the study door for Penelope, and followed her through the vicarage and into the garden.

Penelope had frequently accompanied, or watched, grown-ups being 'shown round' gardens. They made small delighted discoveries as they walked, and now and then their host or hostess would modestly invite their attention to something they had missed. Penelope felt this should be happening on the present occasion. But Caspar Ferneydale said nothing at all. He strolled along in an absent-minded way which she was sure wasn't meant to be rude, but which was disheartening, all the same. It occurred to her to wonder whether he was a philosopher, and happiest when shut up alone with a great many bumper books and a favourite cat. Philosophers, however, were usually rather old, whereas Caspar was almost as young as a fully-grown person can be. Still, he must be eighteen or nineteen, and it was perfectly possible that he was exactly twice her own age. Skirting the lily-pond near the bottom of the garden, Penelope worked it out that one person could be just twice the age of another person only at a single moment in his life. That was one of the funny things about time. If Caspar really was a philosopher, or even intended to become one at the appropriate age, would he be interested if she told him that her father proposed one day to write a book about Time—and sometimes talked to her on the subject in a very deep and incomprehensible manner? She had almost embarked on this disclosure when it came to her that her father mightn't like this cherished plan of his to be generally known. Perhaps it was a family secret—like her Aunt Maud, who was mad and shut up in some kind of hospital.

'There used to be goldfish,' Penelope said rather desperately. 'In this lily-pond, I mean. They were supposed to amuse me and my friends, and we had to feed them with smelly little pellets. You can't really do much with fish. Except just look.'

'That's very true, Penelope. They're a remote and isolated creation, the finny tribe.'

'What do you mean, please: the finny tribe?'

'It's poetry for "the fish". Just as "the feathered songsters of the grove" is poetry for "the birds".'

'*Good* poetry?' Asking this, Penelope glanced at Caspar askance.

'Bad.' Caspar was interested to see that the child received this verdict with satisfaction, as if reassured that he wasn't teasing her. 'And what happened to the goldfish?' he asked. 'Were they eaten by the cat?'

'Of course not! That would be horrid.'

'Not at all. What cat's averse to fish? That's poetry too—and a good deal better.'

'Do you know a lot of poetry, Mr Ferneydale? Do you and your brother recite it at home?'

'We certainly don't do *that*. It wouldn't be appreciated. And Fulke, as a matter of fact, says he hates poetry.' Caspar saw that Penelope was shocked by this. 'What *did* happen to the goldfish?' he asked quickly.

'Well, they *were* eaten, and it *was* rather horrid. A heron came and swallowed all of them. It flew down three days running, and just stood in the pond until the silly things came near enough to be gobbled up. When it went away for the last time it was so full of fish that it could hardly flap itself into the air. Papa was cross with Mr Ferris—Mr Ferris is our gardener—for not netting the pond after the first time. Do you think it would have been fair to do that, Mr Ferneydale?'

'That's a very hard question.' It was clear that Caspar said this in a serious and truthful way. 'And please don't call me Mr Ferneydale. It's a ridiculous name, anyway. Call me Caspar, please.'

'But you're a grown-up.'

'My dear Penelope, look round Mallows, and you'll see that you and I are almost the same age. Think of Mrs Hufkins in Willow Cottage, who remembers the Battle of Waterloo. Or of old Mr Botley, who used to wash down stage-coaches in the yard of the Winton Arms. Or of Grannie Elbrow, who was a Londoner once, and sold oranges along with Nell Gwyn at Drury Lane. You'll realize that you and I are as near being kids together as doesn't count.'

'I *am* going to school in September,' Penelope said. She spoke with a sobriety which might have been felt as a rebuke to these absurdities, but in fact they enchanted her. 'And, Caspar, you're at the 'varsity, aren't you, now?'

'Yes, but I'm only just beginning there. By the way, we don't say "'varsity" any longer, Penelope. We say "university".'

'Papa says "'varsity".'

'And not many people say "Papa", either. It seems to be mostly "Daddy" nowadays.' Caspar was aware that these were impertinent remarks, and might be resented. 'But ''varsity', at least, was a bit too archaic to be put up with—except, perhaps, in reports of football matches—and he didn't like to think of this nice girl being laughed at when she went curtseying into school, uttering outmoded words like a character strayed out of an Edwardian novel.

'Will you tell me more about dolphins, please?' Penelope had moved on from the lily pond, and at the same time had changed the subject thus with mature composure. 'I've only seen them in picture-books. Do they have a great deal of fun?'

'I think it quite likely that they do.'

'Because Cleopatra says Antony's delights were dolphin-like. I don't know quite *what* delights. Do you?'

'Well, he seems to have enjoyed all sorts of things. Fighting, for instance. And making speeches.'

'Oh, yes—speeches. It's in the speeches-from-Shakespeare book I sometimes read with Mrs Martin. They showed his back above the element they lived in. That makes you see a dolphin.'

'Better than you see Mark Antony, perhaps.' Caspar was impressed by this odd evidence of precocity in Penelope's present education. 'Long ago, people used to say the dolphin is the king of the fish, just as the lion is the king of the beasts, and the eagle of the birds. It was rather a good choice, because we know now that dolphins aren't

44

just frolicsome. They're very clever indeed. If they didn't happen to live in water—which we've agreed is rather thwarting—they'd probably be running things on this planet now instead of us.'

'Why are the dolphins very clever?' Penelope had given the strange and mildly alarming information she had just received due consideration before asking this pertinent question. 'There can't be a great many things to do with cleverness, down there in the sea. Except avoid octopuses.'

Caspar had no answer to this mystery—or at least none in terms of the ceaseless operation of the Divine Abundance, the only area in which, at this period, he thought it profitable to seek one. So he offered, without enthusiasm, what he supposed to be a Darwinian explanation. Dolphins had gone through hard times—probably for several million years—and it had marvellously sharpened their wits. They might be regarded—he added with an irresistible start of fancy—as the Jews of the watery element.

Penelope received this respectfully, but didn't seem very impressed. Caspar found himself hoping that she hadn't got him typed as somebody exclusively concerned to talk nonsense. He oughtn't, perhaps, to have produced that stuff about the Battle of Waterloo and Nell Gwyn's oranges. Being funny wasn't at all his true line; he left that to Fulke. It was just that he hadn't wanted to be positively dull with the child. Her home couldn't be exactly a sparkling concern. He hoped that Mr Rich had chosen a thoroughly lively school for his daughter. But that was something the old snob was likely to have done only through inadvertence.

They inspected the unfinished tennis court, and Penelope said there was a promise that it would be ready for play within a few weeks.

'And Daddy,' she added, 'is going to give me a short lesson every day. He says there are some things it's very important to do properly right from the beginning.'

'I expect you'll come on like anything.' 'Daddy' had quite startled Caspar, and he was also impressed by such evidence of paternal devotion on Henry Rich's part. Perhaps the vicar *had* chosen a lively school. One must remember, Caspar told himself, that even Anglican clergymen are also God's creatures. 'I've played tennis once or twice with your father,' he said. 'He's pretty good. You have to get him running about the court, or you haven't a chance.'

45

'He says it's going to keep him fit—our tennis court, I mean. And it's nice that it will be ready before what's so dull a part of the year for him. It's a long time, you see, between the point-to-point and the pheasants. If it hadn't been for John Knox and people, he says, he might be a bishop in Scotland and have the grouse from the glorious twelfth. I don't know what the glorious twelfth is. But I think he's making some sort of joke.'

'It's the twelfth of August. And yes—I believe he must be.' Caspar was trying to remember whether there were any clerics just like the vicar of Mallows in Trollope. Or possibly in Peacock? Mr Rich seemed to belong even further back than either.

'I expect you and your brother don't find an awful lot to do in the country,' Penelope said. The interest of the tennis court being exhausted, they were now returning to the vicarage. 'Do you still swim in the little lake in your park?'

'Yes, Fulke and I sometimes do.' Caspar was surprised by this sudden question.

'Isn't it rather muddy and duckweedy? I remember seeing you once—but ever so long ago.'

'It's all right for swimming, and even for a clean dive in one or two places. But if one gets fooling around it does turn a bit mucky.' Caspar gave these replies while considering the slight oddity of what he had been told. Fulke and he invariably bathed naked, and he could recall two or three occasions upon which village girls had bobbed up at a wary distance and laughed and shouted in a plebeian but not wholly ungratifying way. But he had no memory at all of what had no doubt been a more mannerly spectatorship on the part of a small girl from the vicarage. Nor was Penelope recalling the incident in other than the most matter-of-fact way now. 'You know,' he said impulsively, 'nowadays people are beginning to go in a great deal for their own outdoor swimming-pools. Filtered and warmed-up and with diving-boards and so on. I think we'd better have my father get busy on one at the Hall. You and your friends could come swimming there. In fact we'd have parties.' Caspar was astonished to hear himself coming forward with this proposal, since he didn't really feel that life at the Hall would be rendered more agreeable by the periodic importing of a bevy of brats in pigtails.

'I suppose that would be mixed bathing,' Penelope said.

'Mixed bathing?' Caspar understood this curious expression, but wondered whether he had ever heard it uttered before. 'Well, yes—I suppose it would. Would you say it was any different from mixed doubles—at tennis, that is?'

'Perhaps my father might. He doesn't like anything fast.'

'Mixed doubles aren't as fast as men's doubles.'

'I don't quite know what he means by fast.' Penelope had very sensibly ignored this confusing of the issue by a feeble joke. 'But he said yesterday to old Mrs Crackenthorpe when she came about the church flowers that he was sorry to notice that there is now a fast set almost within visiting distance of Mallows, although fortunately not actually in our parish.'

Caspar felt that Fulke would have appreciated this accurate piece of reporting. And he almost said, 'A fast set sounds like tennis too.' But he thought better of this, and instead asked, 'Does your father think we're fast at the Hall?'

'Oh, no—not *fast*.' Penelope had put unconscious candour into this emphasis, and Caspar realized that his own recent slight advancement in Henry Rich's esteem was of very little account. The vicar judged people by what had been happening to them in the sixteenth century—and nobody had a notion of what had been happening to Ferneydales in that interesting period. Penelope, moreover, was probably being fed on that ancient-lineage nonsense now, and might have difficulty in managing herself a change of diet as she grew older. Her very name took you back to earls of Essex and Warwick and Holland, and for that matter to Sir Philip Sidney and the lord knew who. And it might be said that she was going to stand in need of a knight, or a knight-errant, herself: one who would rescue her from the dragon's maw of such outmoded social attitudes and release her for a decent life in the modern world.

This extreme view of the matter remained for a little time in Caspar Ferneydale's mind after he had taken leave of the child and walked home. He even felt rather glad that she *was* a child, and not any sort of nubile maiden in distress, so that the knight-erranting would have to be undertaken a good many years ahead and by a younger man. Anything of the sort was no more his line than being funny was. And he doubted (although disposed to dream of fair women) whether he ever wanted a sexual drive to be overmastering in the fashion that is a staple resource of novelists and playwrights. Certainly he didn't want anything of the kind to prompt him to the taking on of tough and distracting assignments of the dragon-killing or even Young-Lochinvar order. Wasn't his speculative position still far from clear to him? Wasn't he becoming conscious that even Father Fisher appeared to point now in one philosophical direction and now in another? Wasn't Europe—and in these days even America—positively spawning sages whose opaque but conceivably momentous revelations required to be tested in depth—in what was at once an exhaustive and an exhausting way?

Perpending some of the more imminently looming of these intellectual exercises, Caspar soon forgot his encounter with the little girl from the vicarage. Penelope, however, was to remember it very well.

III

WITH FULKE FERNEYDALE at this time—the six weeks which Oxford calls its Easter Vacation—sex was much more definitely an immediate concern. Sex was good for all sorts of jokes, but serious questions had to be asked about it. Were his own answers to them going to be like other people's? It was to investigating this that he had decided to dedicate part at least of the long holiday available to him.

In his last years at school Caspar, although dreaming or daydreaming of beautiful girls, had on two or three occasions been involved with younger boys in ephemeral episodes of a juvenile and nakedly concupiscent sort. (It was this activity that had led to his being dubbed, according to Fulke, 'a boot-cupboard type'.) Fulke, on the other hand, had worshipped first one, and then a second, beautiful youth from afar. These had been romantic and chivalric affairs with a high emotional charge. They had been bewildering and even, in a small way, tragic experiences. Certainly they had left Fulke frustrated, uncertain of himself, confronting what he felt to be unsatisfactory possibilities, and very ready to offer Caspar, or any congenial companion, that reductive view of an almost universal human activity summarized in the statement that sex is all balls. He was aware that his attitude as an objective and dispassionate observer of life's comedy, and even as the puppet-master contriving those absurd and malicious experiments, were tied up with something he felt to be equivocal within himself. So now he was organizing a key experiment.

Ideally, he supposed, you find a nice girl, perhaps not virginally inclined but not positively cock-teasing, and you excite yourself about her by heavy petting and so on until you're within an inch of being driven right round the bend. In the nick of time she gets into bed with you. And then—either straight away or after a boss-shot or two—you are having a marvellous and utterly indescribable physical experience. This, by all accounts, was the basis of the whole thing, and ought clearly to be tackled as soon as possible. If it proved to be a fraud—if it turned out that for some people, including himself, it was a bad joke—one would feel a proper Charlie, no doubt. But at least one would know, and there was always strength in knowledge.

Just this experiment, however, would take time to mount. Months might go by before you found, and successfully chatted up, the proper girl. Even on theoretical grounds, moreover, it might be better to begin more cautiously at the bottom of the ladder. The experiment, in its purity, required that you should be in no danger whatever of falling into the mysterious and unhappy state (which he knew about) of being in love. In other words, he had better start off with a professional.

Yet there were objections to this course. Fulke had read numerous novels—distinctly *démodé*, yet informative in their way—in which a very young man, tormented by images of fleshly desire rather cautiously intimated by the author, is carried off by a prostitute into what proves to be an episode either of appalling fiasco and humiliation, or of simply no significance at all: a non-event as one might say if feeling linguistically inventive. But fiction aside, Fulke concluded, you obviously stack the cards against yourself if you contrive your experience briskly for five pounds down. There would be too close an association with the price of a decent dinner at the Ritz. You'd probably recall, as you produced the cash, having heard a labourer in a pub say he'd rather have, any day of the week, a good square meal—and having known at once what he was talking about.

But even if he were game to go after the thing in that straightforward commercial way (and he didn't see why not) it was still true that he somehow couldn't see himself picking up a lurking girl in a side-street in London's West End. He might run into somebody quite catastrophic—say his tutor or an aunt—in the very moment of doing so! Fulke, who rather prided himself in possessing (like Henry James, as he had somewhere read) the 'imagination of disaster', even found this endowment alarmingly operative when he sketched such an episode prelusively in fantasy. The thing always took a dreadful turn. It would prove, for instance, actually to be one of his aunts—reputed a most respectable woman—who was soliciting his custom.

He was well aware of the absurdity of all this; of its presenting him, as in a mirror, with an unlicked cub sadly at variance with the sophisticated and incisive young man as whom he disguised himself even to his brother Caspar. But at least this spectacle of a mildly dissociated personality was amusing, and he made some notes on it for future use. He was still making them, indeed, on the train that took him from Calais to Paris.

It amused him, too, that what was for Caspar the city of Monsieur Sartre was for him the city of the unknown harlot. He tried this in French, and as a title. *La ville de la putain inconnue.* He nursed for a few minutes a grandiose plan to master French so thoroughly that he could write verse in it with elegance, like T. S. Eliot, or prose like Julian Green. At least his present French was good enough to enable him to make what he conceived to be some necessary purchases in a chemist's shop.

The sexual initiation thus so unpromisingly put in train began as dismally as the sternest moralist could desire. Fulke was so alarmed that he barely looked at his chosen girl until they were engulfed in what he supposed must be *une maison de tolérance.* The girl turned out to be of mature years and not at all good-looking. She also appeared to be in a hurry, and even resisted Fulke's suggestion that she should fully undress. It wasn't, she said, necessary. Fulke was in a hurry of his own, but he was offended, all the same. Indeed, he was humiliated after a fashion in which the moralist would again rejoice, since he was sensitive enough to perceive that here was a kind of vestigial prudery coming into play when a woman in this situation believes herself to be landed with a mere schoolboy or a notably cold fish.

All these depressing circumstances, however, failed to culminate in an edifyingly disillusioning close. For suddenly something latent in Fulke took hold of the situation, so that its squalid and dismal aspects (which were undeniable) became irrelevant, or at least cynically acceptable. It didn't matter that the tart's low moans and little animal cries and so on were probably no more than a routine turn, switched on once she had, for some reason, decided to give him the appearance of his money's worth. What mattered was that in this very specific and utterly physical activity he had discovered himself at a first go to be thoroughly efficient and securely in charge. And although the indescribable was there all right, and to an effect that entirely confused and mingled the physical and heaven knew what, it was still this identifiable sense, a sense of dominance, that was chiefly important.

In something under ten minutes he'd got through what for primitive adolescents in the jungle it takes months of Mumbo-Jumbo to achieve. He'd passed his virility test and joined the warriors of the tribe! There ought to be a little badge to signalize the fact—the equivalent of an ivory skewer or silver ring through lip or nose. The kind of thing coveted by Boy Scouts.

It was on the following morning that this thought came to Fulke, and he got it into his note-book, since it seemed rather neat. But this utilitarian moment wasn't characteristic of his state. He wandered about Paris, Paris in spring, in a kind of muddled euphoria which seemed every now and then to give way to moments of extreme clarity. Two or three times he sat down in a café, ordered *un filtre*, and considered his future as if it were unrolled like a map on the little table before him. What had happened to him on the previous night wasn't going to happen to him a second time; never again, that was to say, would he tumble on a bed with a common whore. He wasn't proposing to be particularly virtuous, but he wasn't going to be a mere low womanizer either. Just as in the writer's craft which was to be his, he'd always be trading up, but not in the vulgar sense of perpetually being on the look-out for a fresh mistress showier than the last. Not that a bit. It would all be a matter of the more and more subtle exploration of the inexhaustibly amazing—as it plainly was—erotic side of life. And it would be in aid of something. It would be quite tremendously that! His note-book would, in a manner of speaking, always be under the pillow. He might become the English Proust.

This last thought got Fulke to his feet in his final café and prowling again—but in a way he vaguely felt to be wastefully self-absorbed and unnoticing when the place he was prowling through was Paris. No—he told himself—he mightn't trade up quite as far as that. In fact he was aware he wouldn't; aware of it with a damaging self-awareness he had come to accept as among the facts of life. But at least he *knew* his Proust, whereas a great many people just talked about him. And every now and then as he walked, and did become alert to his surroundings, it was to pick up random associations from the interminable book. What had been Swann's address in Paris—an address judged so inadequately fashionable by Odette? And ought he not to have a look at the Jardin d'Acclimatation, where the young Marcel had been so proud to walk beside that shady lady?

If this sort of thing hadn't been going through Fulke's head, and if his late adventure hadn't left him in a state more disturbed than he knew, there wouldn't now have befallen him an incident that was very odd indeed. He certainly wasn't in any sort of kids' zoo, he hadn't gone near the Bois, so there was no close topographical link at work. He was simply walking down a broad boulevard—distinctly posh and not much frequented—when there, suddenly, the incredible presence was. He was gazing at her with an acuteness of perception all the more overwhelming in contrast with the exalted woolliness of his previous state. His first persuasion was that she was marvellously dressed in the height of fashion, and his second that she was totally beautiful in rather a queer way. And then he found that he had said to himself on the instant, 'Why, it's Odette de Crécy!' That this was the lady's identity didn't disconcert him, so that afterwards he was to reflect that it was a little like seeing a ghost. He didn't feel surprised or frightened or incredulous, and it is just the absence of such reactions that is remarked by persons acquainted with the literature of supernatural appearances. And certainly he wasn't entertaining himself to a bookish joke. It was simply as if Charles Swann's wife and former mistress were already slightly known to him, and now here she was—precisely where you might expect, any day, to run into her.

An aberration of this kind can't last long. Fulke was just mastering it—although noticing, indeed, that the apparition a few yards in front of him did possess sharp features and out-size eyes—when the apparition, which was standing by a kerb, raised a gloved hand and beckoned to him. Or so Fulke (going off his rocker again, as he later knew it to be) thought. And he now walked straight up to her, and said in English, 'I say, how delightful of you to remember me!' By the time he had achieved this impertinence, he had another and slightly more rational theory in his head. The beckoning lady was to be described not as Odette but as *an* Odette. She was an absolutely top-class courtesan, as remote from his companion of the night as a Field Marshal from a private in the pay corps. And she had taken a fancy to him on sight.

She beckoned again—rather imperiously this time—with the result that a chauffeur-driven limousine which had been parked in a convenient space on the other side of the boulevard now started into motion and within seconds drew up beside her. To Fulke himself there had been no summons at all! This abasing fact had just dawned on him when the lady turned to him and spoke.

'Perhaps'—she said in a very upper-class foreigner's English—'it would be as well if you went home?'

'I haven't got a home. I mean I'm in a hotel. I'm a tourist.' Fulke heard himself say this—and, in particular, utter that last and incredible word—with dull astonishment. There had been an understandable chilliness in her voice. She supposed him to be drunk: a callow English boy on a spree in Paris. It was quite horrible. If he only *had* been drunk, his *gaffe* would have been less unintelligible. Had those three or four *filtres* been three or four *fines*, his behaviour might have been excused. Indeed, it might have been radically better, since he believed himself not too bad at carrying his liquor like a gentleman. As it was, all he could do was to mutter some sort of apology and shamble away. He'd never felt so cheap in his life, and precipitate retreat was the only course open to him.

But before Fulke could manage even this something startling happened. The offended lady, after no more than a further quick glance, slightly raised her chin, and laughed at him. Fulke, although indeed startled, was far from resentful. It couldn't have been called a frank or friendly or good-humoured laugh, but it certainly wasn't rude or crude either. There may have been a hint of mockery in it, but what it chiefly conveyed was a kind of acknowledged complicity in mischief. It was almost as if some telepathic force was at work, conveying to the awareness of this total stranger the fact and even perhaps the quality of Fulke's recent initiation. The laugh lasted only a moment, and was so softly uttered that one could almost have believed one had imagined it. But Fulke had never heard anything so bewitching in all his experience (which was not, indeed, extensive) and he was instantly swung back to the notion that it was unquestionably one of Paris's supreme *filles de joie* or high-life *hetairai* that was in front of him. A woman who with a mere chuckle could do to a man's spine what she was doing to his couldn't have escaped or failed to accept such a destiny.

'Then I think I had better take you there,' the lady said. 'To your hotel, that is. Are you, perhaps, at the Chatham?'

Fulke knew enough about the Chatham to wonder whether this was meant in fun. He was probably looking—he must be looking, after his night on the town—thoroughly scruffy, not to say grotty, and more likely to be shacking up in some student dump on the Left Bank.

'It's called the Daunou,' he said. The Daunou wasn't exactly the Chatham or the Bisson or the Astor. But it was pretty grand, all the same. He rather wished he'd been more modest in his choice.

'I hope it is comfortable—and quiet and discreet?'

'Oh, yes—it's all right.' Fulke had been obscurely perturbed by that last word. Although he knew it to be crazy, he felt that it hinted unutterable things. 'But, really, Madame——'

'Get in, Monsieur.'

The lady was now in her car—it was a Rolls-Royce, and of that badge of Anglophilia there weren't as yet many around post-war Paris—and the chauffeur was standing by with an enormous fur rug. Fulke got in—with surprising address, considering that his head was now swimming badly. The rug instantly extended its charity over both the lady and himself. The sensation, as the Rolls glided into motion, was of being together in a luxurious mobile bed.

'You know Paris well?' the lady asked politely. 'But, no—for all through your boyhood Paris was closed, alas, to our English friends.'

'Well, yes. I haven't had much chance, I'm afraid. I have a brother who knows Paris better than I do. He's a friend of Monsieur Sartre.'

'That is indeed interesting.' The lady had taken a moment to trace this name, leaving Fulke leisure to feel that he had said a supremely idiotic thing. The lady, however, judged it to be merely amusing. Even more briefly and low-breathed than before, the laugh came again. Fulke was aware of shivering all over.

'And the Beaver?' the lady asked. 'Is your brother a friend of hers as well?'

Although Fulke was in a confused state in a general way, his mind was working in patches with commendable speed. English aspirants to French literary society (of whom there were always plenty going) probably didn't commend themselves to it by splashing around English-type nicknames for its members in their familiar talk. This alarming woman, in fact, was tempting him to be rather crass. As if he hadn't been that in a big enough way already!

'I don't know,' he said politely, 'whether my brother has the honour of Madame de Beauvoir's acquaintance.' He was rather pleased with this; it was the same tactic as Caspar's 'Monsieur Sartre'. But he was also increasingly in sheer physical disarray. Was it possible that, under the all-embracing rug, the lady's thigh was pressing lightly against his own? Or had he shifted his own posture in an unmannerly way so as himself to secure this heady contiguity? Or, again, was he merely imagining something, and was some fold of the furry object securely interposed between them?

'Where were you at school?' the lady asked. 'And your brother too, perhaps?' These questions seemed somehow to follow logically upon the discretion Fulke had just exhibited over M. Sartre's distinguished friend. In England, and upon the strength of so short an acquaintance, they would scarcely, perhaps, have been quite the drill. But something had to be allowed to a foreigner, and Fulke gave his answer at once.

'Ah, but yes! I have a nephew at just such a school in England. It is near Windsor.'

Fulke was without any high regard for Eton College. It was an overgrown place, with plenty of decent chaps in the middle, no doubt, but well sandwiched between scum above and dregs below. All the same, this information, if authentic, did seem to dispose of the Odette theory of his companion. Anglomaniac though she was, it was impossible to conceive of the real Odette, whether as Mme Swann or as Uncle Adolphe's 'Lady in pink', accommodated with such a young male relative, and the same must hold of a real-life person in the same profession. So there was only one other explanation of her. He was being conveyed to his destination at the Daunou by one of the veritable *grandes dames* of Parisian society. This needn't, of course, mean that she had missed her vocation in not becoming a nun. Very cautiously, Fulke shifted his right leg a little further to the right. There was nothing there—which was fair enough, the Rolls being the capacious vehicle it was. He *had* been imagining things. So that was the answer to that.

'And here is your hotel,' the *grande dame* said, as the car put on a superb show in the way of rapid but imperceptible deceleration. 'I hope your bedroom is comfortable—and quite undisturbed during the day?'

The word 'bedroom'—not necessarily emotive in itself—effected a further disturbance in Fulke—one of a definitely physiological order. Aware of this stirring, he answered rather wildly.

'Oh, yes,' he said, 'it's not at all bad. Everything rather on the small side, perhaps. But not so that one couldn't make do.'

'Because sleep is what you need, I think.' The laugh had come again, and this time it was more aphrodisiac (for that was the brutal word for it) than ever. 'You speak in English of "sleeping it off", I think?'

'Yes. But—well, I'm not drunk, you know.'

'No, no—not that. Some other experience. An intoxication that is metaphorical, shall we say? A charming encounter, Monsieur. Goodbye.'

Fulke became aware that the door of the car was open; that the chauffeur—he was of the disagreeably impassive sort—had whipped away the rug; and that he himself was meekly scrambling to the pavement. He was aware, too, that the lady was holding out her hand, and in a manner indicating that it was to be kissed, not shaken. He tried to remember about this. Was it correct in France so to perform the action that what you kissed was your own thumb—or was that just some nonsense he had read about Vienna before the Kaiser's War? He took a peck at the lady's glove, and heard the low laugh for the last time. He said something like 'Awfully kind of you', stepped back, and had the presence of mind to add a formal bow. But would an ingenuous wave and a shy grin be more in the picture she had conceived of him? He was still asking himself this question when the car vanished from sight.

Rather to the surprise of both brothers, Fulke gave Caspar a detailed account of these adventures. This didn't happen while they were at home together during the final week of the vacation. For at Mallows their boyhood's habit of a good deal of reticence over intimate matters at once reasserted itself. More than they realized, they remained much under the thumb of the Ferneydale family ethos, which discouraged any emphasis upon the inner mind as a kind of bad form, or at least as something uselessly aside from the practical affairs of life. They both respected their parents' code here, although each was in his own way aware of its deficiencies. It wasn't a particularly burdensome awareness, since they were confident that other worlds awaited them. To these other worlds Oxford was already something more than a halfway house. So at once when they returned there they took up their lately acquired habit of more open communication.

The first colloquy along these lines occurred in Caspar's rooms in New College. These owned an amplitude similar to Fulke's in Christ Church, but were more austere in effect. Veneration was required not for an original salmon-pink lady by Modigliani but for a colour-print of Duccio's *Rucellai Madonna*, and beyond this there was nothing of artistic interest in evidence. Caspar had already amassed a great many books: a substantial minority relevant to what Oxford at that time understood as providing a basis in philosophy, but the great majority being in French and representing *les belles lettres* very much at large. Fulke picked his way around these cautiously, with a care not to pause before unfamiliar names. On the scholarly side of things there could be no doubt that his brother was getting well ahead of him.

'Good Lord, Cass,' he said, 'acres of Gide! A bit old-hat, isn't he, in the *ambiance* of Monsieur Sartre?'

'Rubbish.'

'And all his boring diaries and letters! Christ, man, you should go back to Baudelaire's *Journaux Intimes*.'

'I do, from time to time.'

'And a chap cavorting round so very much *en prince* all on the strength of one halfpennyworth of bread to this intolerable deal of sack. *La Symphonie Pastorale*, and that's about it. Or I'll throw in *La Porte Étroite*.'

'You show every sign of developing into a vulgar sciolist, Fulke. Do you kid yourself you have nothing to learn from *Les Faux-Monnayeurs*?'

'It suggests a method, I admit. Chinese boxes. But it puts him with the trick writers: Pirandello, and the like.' Fulke paused on this, but it was received with the impassive silence by which an examiner in a *viva* marks his sense that a singularly insufficient thought has been enunciated by the candidate before him. 'But I'll tell you,' Fulke went on, 'one thing that has been striking me about the French—about the highly-educated French. It's something, actually, that peeps out in that very novel. Intellectually speaking, they allow their children no childhood at all. They have to be turned into little egg-head adults as if they belonged in a mediaeval world and were more likely than not to die at thirty. At what age did Proust die?'

'I don't know. But he was barely over fifty, I imagine.'

'You could have foretold it from his Marcel.'

'Well, that brings us to what you were beginning to burble about: your chat with Odette. And I'd like to hear about its prelude, please, in all its salacious detail.'

'Then won't you have to tell Father Fisher in his funny little confessional that you have deliberately solicited an impure communication?'

'Yes, of course. And he may have something to say about the delicate balance often operative in such situations. It would be wrong in me to coax images of carnal excitement out of my brother. But it would be equally wrong to turn away from some frailty of which he wanted to disburden himself.'

'It sounds to me like a theory of confession at second hand. Whether I want to disburden myself, I don't at all know. Perhaps I just want to boast. These things are confusing, it can't be denied.' Fulke scowled, as he sometimes did when remembering that the first duty of a serious artist is a searching analysis of experience. 'Anyway, I've told you the brute fact. I went to Paris because I hadn't the nerve to pick up a tart in the West End.'

'I think that was perfectly sensible.' Caspar's gaze was on the Duccio. To pick up a woman of *that* order, he might have been reflecting, you had to go to Florence or Siena. But when he turned back to his brother his body had tautened a little. 'Well?' he said.

'She had to be slapped out of a performance altogether too perfunctory for the money.' Fulke already had this phrase lodged in his note-book; and perhaps from his memory of what he had there further written rather than from straight recollection he went on to say a good deal more. Caspar received the information without interrupting. It bore, perhaps, more of the genuinely informative than it would have done twenty years later, when novelists in particular had taken leave to enliven their pages with copiously explicit material on the activity involved. But presently, of course, Fulke had to dry up, and then Caspar did speak.

'What was she like?'

'I've told you, haven't I? What you might call her proportions were a surprise. Sometimes she seemed to be pretty well all buttocks.'

'Bother her buttocks! What sort of person was she? Where had she come from and where did she think she was going? All that.'

59

'Good heavens, Cass, I haven't a clue.'

'You felt no curiosity about her? Curiosity's understood to be your line.'

'My dear man, it's just not that sort of situation.' When Fulke called his brother 'my dear man' there was commonly something uneasy involved, and in a sense he faced up to this now. 'If anything is entitled to be called the bare bones of a personal relationship it's tumbling a strange woman on an apology for a bed.'

'Bare bones doesn't seem to go with big buttocks.' Caspar scarcely seemed to approve of having contrived this witticism. 'Tell me more about the other thing. I expect you weren't so utterly mindless over your Odette.'

Obediently, Fulke elaborated for some minutes on his encounter with the *grande dame*, and this time Caspar interrupted with several questions.

'You find the Rolls rather less distasteful than the brothel, or whatever it was, don't you?' Fulke eventually asked.

'Definitely not. In fact, I judge your second day to be the nastier of the two. More radically depraved, that is.'

'So that if I'd just pushed a little harder——' Fulke broke off, perhaps recalling his feeble remarks on the possible conveniences of his hotel.

'Nothing of the sort. You weren't within a mile of her, even if she was as vicious as they come. Amusing herself with ten minutes' titillating of a bewildered English boy! The first bitch was at least securing herself her next day's dinner.'

'I take your point.' Fulke said this quite soberly. 'But there, within a few hours of each other, were those two strongly contrasted situations. It was almost a *trouvaille*. Think of getting those two women together, and working out what they'd make of one another.'

'Sole survivors from a shipwreck, isolated on a desert island? Scarcely a novel device.'

'Or stranded just for the night, say, in a mountain hut. Something could be made of it.'

'Certainly it could. But on a basis of intuition and empathy rather than jottings in a note-book. You'd need a whack of Maupassant along with a whack of Proust. Honestly, Fulke, you have to begin thinking seriously about yourself as a writer. About the twitch of your tether, if it's to be brutally put. There's observing, and mucking in with what goes on, I don't doubt. There may even be merit—although I distrust it—in your pet theory of the portable psychological lab. But there's seeing into the life of things, as well.'

'God, Cass, you do set my sights for me! But thanks a lot. It's something, I suppose, to have one of Nature's dons as a brother. And, talking of dons, I've a tute at five, and the bloody essay still to write. So see you again soon.'

IV

HENRY RICH'S RELUCTANCE to despatch his daughter Penelope to boarding-school had presented the appearance of a transitory feeling, unlikely to amount to much. There had been an element of muddle in it. He wasn't clear in his head about how he should apply what he was sure was his just regard for traditional ways of life to the specific problem of the right form of education for boys and girls respectively: this in point both of the range of studies provided and the environment within which the providing should take place. He had also been in a bit of a muddle—surely of an ephemeral sort—about Mrs Martin, an admirable and entertaining woman with whom he would be sorry to lose touch, and with whom he could even imagine himself, if fleetingly, as graduating to touch in a different sense. In this last thought there was a thoroughgoing confusion. He could, if he chose, propose marriage to Mrs Martin upon the very morrow of the day upon which Penelope and her trunk and tuck-box departed together. (That there actually had to be anything so entirely masculine in suggestion as a tuck-box had startled him a good deal.) Alternatively, if he felt indisposed to abandon his now settled predilection for a celibate ministry, there would be no impediment (barring the lady's own mind in the matter) to his enjoying almost as much of Mrs Martin's society as hitherto. Provided a due decorum be observed alike in appearance and fact, there is held to be nothing censurable in an acknowledged warmth of regard between a middle-aged incumbent who is a widower and an all-but middle-aged parishioner who is a widow.

When Penelope did set out—with what in retrospect presented itself as a slightly wounding lack of lamentation on her part—the real problem proved to be different. Mr Rich was confident that she was going to be in good hands. He knew that, assisted at the end by Mrs Martin, he had come to a right decision, and that it was indeed going to be to his child's advantage that she was now to cope with, and doubtless enjoy, a larger society than Mallows afforded. But it soon emerged that he missed her; that he missed her very much. Nor did his sense of having done the right thing here help him greatly. He recalled with dismay that he had sometimes felt his sole responsibility for her as burdensome and even tedious. He had always answered her questions carefully, knowing it to be important that a child's curiosity should be sharpened and enlarged. But it had often been with his mind on other matters; and often, too, he must have chosen his topics of conversation ineptly, and with a sense that the world of Penelope's imagination was closed to him as it ought not to be. There had even been times when he had avoided a walk with her, or the prolonging of a meal, because of the slight tiresomeness of matching one's mind with a child's. Had his own insufficiencies in such matters, his own mere liking for ease, been a lurking element in his decision to shoo her off to school?

He soon discovered, too, that what might have amused the child if casually and immediately reported at the breakfast-table or in the schoolroom could look distinctly flat in a weekly letter. Such a letter, however, he conscientiously wrote every Saturday afternoon without pause after the composition of the following day's sermon. He made a point of mentioning and discussing anything in Penelope's last obligatory letter home that could with any appropriateness be thus taken up. He did this by way of demonstrating that he had read with attention whatever she had to say—but also with the further thought that, as she moved up the school and her powers of rational discourse developed, there might here be a useful vehicle for serious debate between father and daughter on matters easier to venture upon in epistolary communication than in direct dialogue. Mr Rich was inclined to distrust the spontaneity that may lurk in the tongue. He was aware that even in his pulpit a divagation into extemporary utterance had frequently been of unhappy effect.

In the years immediately following upon its installation in the grounds of the vicarage the hard tennis-court proved a considerable success—as was to be expected of a project entered upon on the strength of much prudent consideration. Its previous non-existence was now quite clearly to be discerned as having been, in Mr Rich's own phrase, almost an unsuitable thing. The Ferneydale boys had played on it regularly for a time when at the Hall there had been that trouble with the moles. Their father and the vicar occasionally engaged in a set or two together while Mrs Ferneydale, who was not athletic, looked on from within the shade of an unassuming but agreeable rustic shelter. Mr Rich was much the stronger performer, and was able to congratulate himself on his command of the unobtrusive tact which the discrepancy called for. When the moles had finally been vanquished there were the due return occasions on the grass court at the Hall, so that in this small matter there was a reciprocity proper between the two principal gentlemen's houses in the neighbourhood. And nothing of this became burdensome. Mr Ferneydale was a man of affairs who held his leisure to be limited, and already during their undergraduate years his sons spent a good part of their vacations away from home. They enjoyed, Mr Rich supposed, allowances distinctly above the average, and found numerous opportunities to improve themselves by travel. In former times they would have been held on a tighter rein until suddenly, upon coming of age or thereabout, launched upon some species of Grand Tour. In this particular Mr Rich was willing to see a measure of merit in modern ways, the annals of his family affording numerous instances of undesirable consequences succeeding upon too abrupt a transition to liberty in such regards.

He still didn't quite approve of Fulke and Caspar. But Caspar at least, whose unsignalled apostasy to the Romish persuasion had once so offended him, had been gaining in his estimation. Caspar was clearly booked for an Oxford fellowship, which is a respectable thing, and he could converse seriously but with a courteous observance of what a plain country parson (albeit of ancient lineage) could be expected to be keeping up with. Fulke, on the other hand, was now generally known to be determined on a literary career, and Mr Rich, who found much to dislike in the tone of contemporary literature, was unfavourably impressed by this ambition. It was true that Fulke's manners were seldom at fault, and that he could be amusing, when prompted that way, irreproachably within the limits of polite conversation. But at the same time he had a strong tendency to ironic and even sarcastic utterance, which the vicar judged a habit of mind particularly to be deprecated in a very young man.

The tennis court fulfilled another of its proposed functions. During the school holidays it provided an attraction both for such local friends as Penelope had and—increasingly as she moved up the school—for several entirely suitable form-mates with whose parents Mr Rich was very content to agree upon an exchange of visits. Yet the presence of these young house-guests, of whom there might sometimes be two, or even three, at a time, was not without its problems in a household over which no lady presided. There were several public-school boys roughly of Penelope's age within hail of Mallows, and to these it would have been unreasonable not to extend invitations on a tennis-party basis. On such occasions Mr Rich generally contrived that Mrs Martin or some similar parishioner should be present to preside over tea. But at other times his widowed condition generated (or at least so he believed) certain awkwardnesses of a domestic sort with which his housekeeper, the promoted cook, had to cope as well as she could. Things would be easier when Penelope was old enough to be the unquestioned mistress of the household. But by that time she might reasonably be looking forward to marriage within a short space of years, and when that marriage took place the life of the vicarage would change in unpredictable ways. Mr Rich sometimes reflected that it would have been different had he been left with a son. He never felt he quite understood Penelope—although it would have puzzled him to give any very precise definition to this expression. A child of one's own sex would presumably be easier to understand, and certainly to plan for in an informed way. Moreover he was aware, if vaguely, that in a man's relationship with a daughter, mysterious though she may be, there can develop an element of dependence less likely to establish itself in his relationship with a son. When eventually he lost Penelope to a husband the deprivation might prove sharper in effect than if he were parting with a son to a wife.

It is improbable that one so good natured as Henry Rich ever remotely betrayed to his daughter even a passing wish that she had been a boy. But it is not improbable that Penelope herself—and at an early age—divined that something of the sort was at least occasionally in her father's head. She might have inferred it, indeed, from the very punctiliousness with which he asserted her femininity. But this, fortunately, didn't take extreme forms. He was far from feeling that a girl should in any degree be debarred from active pursuits. He had even tried to teach her a little cricket, and when this had failed of success he dissimulated his impatience very well. When she was at home he was careful to advance her horsemanship as well as her tennis; and from school he liked to hear of her progress at lacrosse.

Penelope herself continued to like tennis best. She practised hard, and watched her father's game closely, taking pleasure in a proficiency which she supposed to be remarkable in one of his advanced years. It was this that made her so promptly aware of the full portentousness of an event that took place hard upon her fourteenth birthday. Mr Ferneydale, that undistinguished performer, beat the Reverend Henry Rich 6–2, 6–0. This was on the vicarage court. And about a week later it became known that a similar issue had succeeded upon a return encounter at the Hall.

The vicar was very annoyed. He was even more annoyed when his daughter, upon an instant's decision and without speaking what she knew would be an unavailing word, called in the family doctor. Dr Hurcomb didn't leave his patient before convincing him that Penelope had been right. Some small thing had happened inside Mr Rich's head. It need not be serious; it must by no means be regarded as premonitory of certain disaster to come. Men had been known to scale Everest, to walk round the North Pole, years after such an episode. Still, there were precautions to be observed.

When news of this got abroad, a number of people announced that for some time they had felt the vicar to be wearing not too well. He preserved, indeed, the appearance of a thoroughly robust man, but to the more perceptive eye, and reflective mind, there had been evident cause for concern. Always of sanguine complexion, he had of late become more noticeably florid. He had also been putting on weight. His very agility on the tennis court (itself the product of perhaps injudicious effort) had only pointed the fact that he was a shade lumbering at other times: in danger, as he himself had been heard to express it, of becoming too heavy for the saddle. Nobody ventured to suggest that he possibly drank more than he should—but this, as it happened, was the only unwise conduct of which he was willing privately to accuse himself. It had something to do with the emptiness of the vicarage during his daughter's absences at school. He had always been inclined a little to linger over his port at the dinner-table; latterly he had formed the habit of carrying his glass and the decanter back with him to his study thereafter. This undesirable practice he confessed to Dr Hurcomb, who promptly made light of it, while at the same time advising its discontinuance. Dr Hurcomb, in his inner mind, thought it still improbable that Henry Rich would fail of that almost excessive longevity which distinguishes the clergy as a class. But it might well be that a little caution before the portals of Bacchus would minimize the risk (which he believed also to be a professional one) of a decade or more evidencing a certain desuetude of the intellectual faculties.

Mr Rich, who liked to be alive and breathing, was willing to be cautious, in both this and other regards. He even undertook a serious review of the bent of his activities as a whole; of his 'life-style', as it was coming to be called. The image of the country gentleman which he had inherited from his family had conceivably too much commanded him, to the neglect of interests and activities for which he believed himself to be authentically, if modestly, endowed. He had lately read a popular if slightly arcane book entitled *An Experiment with Time*, and been reminded of his own more philosophic interest in the mysterious fact that all things flow. He began to make fuller use of his dining-rights at his Oxford college (at which Caspar Ferneydale had now become some sort of postgraduate student) and to converse whenever he could with those of the dons whom he judged likely to fructify his own thinking in this field. He thus threatened to become something of a menace, and was even occasionally referred to (very absurdly) as Little Father Time. But he was generally felt to be sufficiently a period piece to be acceptable around the place. People liked, too, his evident enjoyment of other aspects of high-table and common-room life. '*Tempus pater*,' a college wit said, 'is without doubt *edax*, although happily not *ferox*, when set before a good square meal.'

But time, although possibly to be experimented with, itself experiments without pause. There can be no fable in which it is not exhibited at work.

Part Two

V

'WHAT SORT OF people,' Dora Quillinan asked, 'live in your Big House?'

'People called Ferneydale.'

'Penelope, you do go in for the most uninformative answers. What do I learn from that one?'

'Probably that they're not in the peerage, and so can't be made fun of on that account.'

It was true that Dora Quillinan was given to extracting amusement from the spectacle of the English social hierarchy. She had asked her question as if it were in the nature of things for everybody to have neighbours in a Big House, and for mild absurdity to inhere in the fact. Dora was clever and rather commanding, and these endowments had resulted in her lately having become Head Girl of Penelope's school. So at this point Penelope might have asserted that Head Girl and Big House were terms belonging to an identical vulnerable vocabulary, satirically regarded. If this was not quite open to her it was because, were she to elect to remain at school throughout her eighteenth year, she would almost certainly become Head Girl herself. Her headmistress would not with any emphasis have declared Penelope Rich to be either commanding or outstandingly clever. But she had decided that Penelope possessed character—an attribute less easily defined—and would at least be an interesting girl to set in authority for a while. Penelope was alert enough to have spotted that she was already being groomed for the position. Whether she thought much of the idea she didn't yet clearly know. It would please her father, which was something. And it would, of sorts, be a test. That life is much a matter of tests was a proposition that she accepted without question.

The two girls were close friends, and Dora had never stayed at the vicarage before because her father was in the Diplomatic Service and owned a *penchant* for holding posts abroad, so that during school holidays she was whisked off to distant corners of the globe—which was something that aeroplanes were increasingly making a matter of common form. But during the present summer her father had been given a desk in the Foreign Office—a term pleasingly misleading in suggestion, this one—and Dora had come to spend a fortnight with the Riches. Mr Rich was gratified to have beneath his roof the daughter of a man before whom ambassadorial status in Paris or Washington was said to be looming up.

'Have these Ferneydales been at your Big House for long?'

'It isn't all that big, as you will presently discover. But, yes—ever since I can remember.'

'That's most impressive.'

'Mr Ferneydale is some sort of business man. But only demi-semi self-made. Public school from his cradle, and all that. Daddy quite likes him, I think, so we see a good deal of the family from time to time. Mrs Ferneydale is dim, but nice. There are two sons: young men, I suppose, although I think of them as middle-aged bachelors. They're not around a lot. Fulke and Caspar Ferneydale.'

'*Fulke* Ferneydale? The dramatist?'

'Yes, that's him.' Penelope was surprised by this sharp question. As something of a purist, linguistically considered, she doubted whether 'dramatist' was quite right for somebody who had enjoyed precocious acclaim with a couple of West End plays. 'He turns up every now and then, but isn't much approved of by the Mallows world in general. Daddy prefers Caspar, who is felt as not being a great success. He is very learned, and got a fellowship at Oxford. But it turned out to be of a kind you hold only for a few years, and then they tell you to move on. Caspar edits a magazine. Or a journal, rather, which probably means less money. It's Catholic, in a vague way, and full of religion and philosophy.'

'Why isn't Fulke much approved in the back-woods?'

'Daddy says he's fast.'

'What a weird expression! It must be Edwardian.'

'Victorian, as a matter of fact. I've heard he's also what was called a *roué*. I came across a *roué* mentioned in *Jane Eyre*. A young *roué* of a *vicomte*—a brainless and vicious youth. I think it was something like that.'

'Fulke Ferneydale can't be brainless.'

'Obviously not. Unlike my father, I find him attractive.'

'Good heavens, Penelope! Don't tell me you're no longer fancy-free.'

'But I'm not. My heart is not wholly untouched, I confess. But it's not by Fulke Ferneydale. Shall I tell you my secret, Dora? It's by Tommy.'

'Who on earth is Tommy?'

'There he is, just over the hedge.' The two girls were in the vicarage garden. 'He's Tommy Elbrow, our new garden boy. Snub-nosed and freckled and fifteen. Every night I dream of his slim clean limbs.'

'Clean limbs? Tommy doesn't look to me as if he baths all that often. What about telling him you intend to give him a good scrub down? It would be an approach.'

Penelope and Dora talked occasional nonsense of this sort, no doubt because aware of themselves as standing with reluctant feet where the brook and river meet. Not that Penelope, at least, would have been likely to suggest to anybody the Maidenhood of Long-fellow's poem. Primly girlish in childhood, she was distinctly boyish now. This was partly a matter of attitude and manner, which were perhaps not uninfluenced by that suppressed preference which she had long ago thought to detect in her father. But there was something physical about the suggestion as well: subtle rather than patent, and certainly far from displeasing. Dora Quillinan, on the other hand, was physically as feminine as could be, and had become aware of her destiny as attractive to all manner of wholesome-minded men. She was far from sure that she rejoiced in this. On the strength of a distant view of the society within which her parents revolved she had become aware of much time-wasting manoeuvre in that region of behaviour. Dora intended to have a career, but not at the expense of allowing herself to be pestered by predatory males, however unchallengeable their more obvious qualifications might be.

'Does Tommy do everything? He must be a devoted and indust-rious youth if he does.' Dora said this as she moved with a pair of secateurs from one rose-bed to another, since the girls were gathering flowers for the house.

'My father is a considerable gardener, and an old man called Mr Mace comes for one day a week. But Mr Mace will use nothing more newfangled than a sickle and a scythe and an old-fashioned push-along mower. Tommy understands machines of one sort and another, and can make their little engines work. Perhaps that's why he looks a bit smudgy. And he tells me he now has almost enough money to buy himself a motor-bike as soon as he's allowed to ride one.'

'You really do sound quite interested in your Tommy.'

'He's at least a figure in the landscape. I'm afraid you'll find life here terribly quiet, Dora. After all the glitter and the gold.'

'I don't give a fig for the glitter and the gold, or resent the fact that I'm still expected to enjoy only a kind of nursery view of them.'

'Before coming out, and so forth?'

'I expect there will have to be a bit of that. But my parents are fairly reliable, and at least won't lay it on thick. It's basically disgusting, you know—suddenly having the clothes ripped from your shoulders and being paraded as now beddable before a crowd of inane young men in white ties.'

'Well, yes. I think I'd be imagining their impertinent paws on me. But perhaps it's not quite like that. One might just suddenly find oneself seriously in love. And have to face up to it.'

'You make it sound like having to go to the dentist, Penelope.'

'Maidenly fears, and all that. Do you know? My father already talks about that coming-out business for me. It will mean rustic revels in houses judged to be of sufficient consequence in this corner of the world, and cadging in on grand relations for a few balls in London—at which I'll feel I'm undertaking the part of third dairymaid in a comedy.'

'Or a modest daffadowndilly strayed in among the exotic blooms in a hothouse.' Dora Quillinan offered her amplification helpfully, and the two girls glanced at one another with satisfaction. Both of them enjoyed this sort of vivacity—Penelope in particular, who went short of anything of the kind on her home ground.

'Doesn't it make a difference, Dora, now that you're sure of that place at Somerville?'

'My dear kid, Oxford is said to be quite frightful nowadays—at one of the women's colleges, I mean. Ever since after the war, it seems, the male undergraduates have taken to acknowledging the existence of their female counterparts. And all the old rules have broken down. They positively *roam* the conventual quadrangles, and you are totally unprotected from them. They themselves at least have bedrooms they can hide in. But there you are in your minute bed-sitter—and suddenly there is an almost strange young man squatting on the floor, watching you mending your stockings or washing your hair. No, the only true refuge is a convent—and convents are probably going that way too.'

'You could buy yourself a pair of steel-rimmed spectacles, and have something perfectly frightful done to your teeth.'

'What about Somerville or LMH for you yourself, Penelope? What would your father say?'

'He wouldn't clamp down on it. But he'd like to think that the only floor-squatters permitted were the young nobility from Christ Church, or, at a pinch, scions of the authentic landed gentry from his own New College.'

'Whereas they'd probably be boys like your Tommy, who've been smart enough to snap out of motor-bikes and into mortar-boards. I think I could like a young man of that sort. He'd have shown there was some stuffing to him.' Dora produced this sentiment with conviction. 'Don't you agree?'

'Well, yes—in theory. But I'd always be inclined to feel he was short of that bath.'

Such a candid confession of prejudice on the part of Mr Rich's daughter interested as well as amused Miss Quillinan, who recalled her friend as having made a speech of a strongly egalitarian persuasion at the school debating society. That had perhaps reflected the robust mind of Penelope's former governess, of whose alliance with an engine-driver's family she had been afforded the history. This immediate remark must be more a matter of paternal inheritance. Dora didn't doubt that the hymn beginning *All things bright and beautiful* was regularly required to be sung with proper conviction in Mallows parish church. It was the one with the bit about the rich man in his castle and the poor man at his gate.

'Then as you're not serious in saying that your heart is touched by Tommy-over-the-hedge, just what sort of person is it really going to be that captures the citadel?'

'What an odd conversation we're having, Miss Quillinan! When I was small I used to say he was going to be a poet—or, failing that, a deep thinker about the ultimate mystery of things.'

'Like this Caspar Ferneydale you were talking about?'

'I wasn't talking about him, but just mentioning him briefly. I'm sure that as a candidate he has never entered my head. But all that was childish nonsense. It's difficult even to begin to think about the kind of man one could square up to marrying.' Penelope sounded quite serious now. 'One knows so little about how they come, anyway.'

'One knows about immediate physical attraction. That's said to be extremely important.'

'Yes, of course. But I don't believe it would stand up by itself for long.'

'More lasting are the qualities of the mind.'

'You can put it that way. I'd want a man who was spontaneous and uncomplicated.' Penelope paused on these brief specifications, which had apparently bobbed up unexpectedly. 'And innocent,' she suddenly added.

'Virginal, you mean? A young hero as yet unknown to woman?'

'Not that at all. And what I do mean I don't clearly know. Let me begin showing you my father's most prized blooms. There's one clematis in particular.'

'That will be a delight. But we mustn't rush things. Let's just walk.'

'Very well. We'll give these flowers to Tommy to take back to the house, and then we'll go round the park.'

'Of Ferneydale Court, or whatever it's called? That's in order?'

'Very much so. Mr Ferneydale is a great hand at being a good squire. He even keeps a whole cricket field in trim for the lads of the village. When they were younger his sons were required to organize matches agreeably mingling the classes of society.'

'But they then rebelled?'

'I think Caspar did. Fulke was rather fond of the hayseed youth. Daddy felt he had to disapprove of his introducing some of them to pub life as soon as they looked old enough for the publican and the local bobby not to feel uneasy. There's some sort of law about the age at which boys can begin propping up the bar in the interval of playing darts.'

Tommy Elbrow accepted his instructions with alacrity, although whether because his own heart was not untouched by Penelope it would have been hard to say. He may simply have felt that he had a career in the making, and that prompt obedience to commands must lead to advancement and a nearer prospect of the motorbike. The girls meanwhile crossed a stile and were on Ferneydale ground, with immediately before them a paddock given over in considerable number to aged and unshorn rams. These superannuated creatures tottered aimlessly around, seemingly alike overburdened by their dingy woolliness and the trailing enormousness of what it would have been absurd to call their private parts.

'I've seen rams in small flocks like this before,' Dora said. 'It seems odd. One knows that a single bull goes a long way.'

'If it isn't too indelicate, you can ask Mr Ferneydale about it when you meet him. He has a great opinion of himself as a practical farmer, Daddy says, and likes to show that he knows all the answers. There's the Hall, over on the left. You can see it more clearly lately, because they've had to cut down several trees. One chunk dates from the fifteenth century, and it has been put together in bits and pieces thereafter in the approved way. But I have a book on English country houses that calls the result "in this instance distinctly inharmonious". Mr Ferneydale wouldn't like that at all. We'll go round on the right. I don't care for the notion of being raked from its windows.'

'By Messrs Fulke and Caspar?'

'Oh, them! As I think I've told you, they're hardly ever around nowadays. But Mrs Ferneydale would come out and do beckoning wavings.'

This change of direction took them not round but across the park, with the result that in a few minutes they were dropping downhill towards the little lake.

'I say—that's nice! It looks as if you could swim in it.' Dora had paused to admire this unexpected amenity.

'Oh, yes. People do.'

'So that must be a bathing hut.' Dora was moving forward again at a quickened pace.

'Yes. It's something fairly recent.'

'And the water must be quite deep, because there's a diving board. Do they let you swim in it?'

'The Ferneydales? I suppose they would. But I never have.'

'Oh, look!' They were now close to the water's edge, and with these conveniences directly in front of them. But Dora's exclamation had been occasioned by something more. They no longer had the scene to themselves. The door of the hut had opened and a young man had appeared in it, plainly prepared for a swim.

'That's Fulke,' Penelope said. 'And here we are, caught gaping. Bother!'

Miss Quillinan saw no reason to be bothered, and said words to that effect. But Penelope wasn't listening. She had recalled something with so sharp an awareness that she had to tell herself it was not now precisely as it had been long ago. Caspar Ferneydale was not present. And Fulke was not entirely naked, since he was wearing a bright red and very tight-fitting bathing slip. Penelope, who owned a certain frankness of imagination, found herself—most ludicrously—thinking of those rams. Only Fulke Ferneydale wasn't decrepit. On the contrary he looked—at this middle-distance, at least—even younger than his years, which Penelope knew quite accurately to be twenty-seven. And now he had run down the little spring-board, taken a practised jump, and disappeared into the pool with scarcely a splash. It was only when he bobbed up again, the water streaming from his hair, that he became aware of his performance as having been observed.

'Penelope,' he shouted, '*benvenuto!* And just wait.'

This had been cordial, but was a command—perhaps because Penelope Rich was, after all, still a kid. Fulke followed it by striking out across the pool, and within seconds he was scrambling out on the bank beside her. The spot was muddy, and trickles of muddy water ran down his thighs as he shook himself. There was a strand of duckweed in his hair. River gods, she thought, had probably looked like this: authentic divinities after a fashion, but with a touch of earthiness to them.

'Hullo, Fulke,' she said—taking the initiative, and now in a brisk tone of the most unbothered sort. 'Dora, this is Mr Fulke Ferneydale. My friend Dora Quillinan, Fulke. Dora is staying with us at the vicarage.'

'How do you do?' It might have been said that Fulke spoke with a slight sense of fun at all this correctness. 'I'll have to save up the handshake, I'm afraid, until I can grab a towel. This pond is very much in a state of nature. And it can remain surprisingly chilly at least for most of the year. Very far from being a *piscine acclimatisée*, which is why we don't use it for sociable splashings.' Fulke glanced swiftly but easily at the girls in turn—starting with Dora. 'But why don't you both come and swim one day? It would be very nice if you did, and I don't expect that either of you would mind a tadpole or two in your hair. You mayn't have brought bathers with you, Miss Quillinan. But I'm sure Penelope has a whole stack of them in a drawer.'

This oncomingness on the part of the successful playwright was momentarily felt as awkward by the girls. But 'Miss Quillinan' seemed to speak of an intention to treat them both as entirely grown-up. And if Fulke's glance, having returned to Dora, was a little lingering on her, there was no sense of a take-it-for-granted boldness about his proposal, which had come with a pleasing undertone of tentativeness and lightness of air.

'I think we might like to,' Penelope said—briskly again, even if with a cautious reliance upon the conjectural mode. 'Tadpoles are all right, but I'd jib at finding I was swallowing a frog. Is Caspar at home with you?'

'Caspar has gone to Paris, to listen to some moribund sage delivering an *éloge* on one who's definitely dead.' It was now on Penelope that Fulke's gaze lingered. 'It must have been a long time since I've seen you,' he said.

'Not really all that long. Going by the calendar, that is. But my father keeps on telling me that time is a very rum affair.' It was now Penelope who was taking a good look at Fulke. She decided she was noticing things she hadn't noticed before, although they must have been progressively there for the remarking over a considerable period. At this closer view Fulke Ferneydale no longer looked younger than his years. In fact, he looked a good deal older than twenty-seven. There were lines—almost wrinkles—round his eyes, and surely something had happened, too, to his mouth. She hadn't seen or read his plays, but understood them to be light-hearted affairs, only just tinged by a modish and undisturbing cynicism. She hadn't heard much about him either. Except, of course, those dark hints concerning the *roué* business. And they, taking account of the sort of informants she had, might mean no more than that he had been sowing a few wild oats in his spare time. No doubt she ought to feel disapproval on that account. Only she didn't. She recalled Dora's piece of rubbish about a young hero as yet unknown to woman, and had to wonder whether

79

what she did feel was a faint jealousy. She reminded herself that she was an unformed and uninformed schoolgirl, with no business to traffic in such notions. But when she had told Dora that she found Fulke Ferneydale attractive she had, she realized, stated an undoubted fact.

'One could put up with time being rum,' Fulke said, 'if it wasn't also invincible. Art is supposed to defy time. Absolute nonsense. The marble crumbles, the pigments flake, the languages die and their words shrivel. "But thy eternal beauty shall not fade." Don't believe it. We can't even be sure whether Shakespeare is celebrating a girl or a boy. Caspar, incidentally, once had a conversation with your father about time. How is your father, Penelope?'

The vicar's daughter made a suitable reply, and added that her father would soon be awaiting his lunch, so that she and Dora had better return home. If Fulke took this as a hint he handled it in his own way—his interest in these all but adult schoolgirls being apparently far from exhausted.

'I'll walk with you as far as the stile,' he said casually. 'And dry out in the sun.'

So this now happened—Fulke placing himself, as if for convenience of talk, between his companions as they set out. Dora took this in her stride, which the young man didn't permit to be of more than a leisured sort. Penelope thought they must appear an odd trio to anybody glimpsing them from afar: two girls in their trim countrified clothes flanking this nearly naked (and agreeably bronzed) male. Fulke, she supposed, must now be an affluent and roving person, who had recently arrived home from some lavishly sun-bathing spot like Biarritz or Antibes.

'Tell me about your school,' Fulke said. 'I don't believe I even know its name.'

Dora had to supply this want. Penelope had remained silent in some displeasure. Had Fulke said, 'I've actually forgotten its name,' the effect might have been a little cavalier, but otherwise unremarkable. He had made it sound, however, as if he never had known the name of her school, and this was impossible. So it somehow felt as if he had found himself short of a further topic of conversation with these schoolgirls, and had reached out for one in rather a random way. But now he became animated again at once.

80

'What an extraordinary thing!' he said. 'I actually have an aunt who is one of your governors. I think she's called a governor and not a governess—which would be more exact, in a way. She must be an old girl, I suppose. Her name is Dewar: Lady Dewar. Her husband is a great big grocer. Do you know her?'

'We don't know much about all that.' This time it was Penelope who replied. 'We're an old-fashioned school, and don't go in for pupil-representation, and that sort of thing.' Penelope felt this to be faintly snubby as she said it, but was merely feeling that Lady Dewar the grocer's wife didn't sound a very promising pivot for further talk. 'Do you think all boarding-schools should go co-educational?' she asked.

'I rather think I do.' Fulke Ferneydale gave this answer with care, as if it were a question to which he had devoted thought without arriving at a definite conclusion. 'And Oxford and Cambridge colleges, too—although that seems a very remote possibility indeed.'

'Some people,' Dora said, 'judge that it would promote premature romance.'

'Romance can't be premature, Miss Quillinan. Laugh at them when they tell you that. What can be premature is signing on for a lifetime's domesticity. So I'd make one proviso about being a co-ed. Don't marry the boy, or girl, at the next desk. It's even more risky than marrying your opposite number next door.' Fulke paused on this, and Penelope—entirely to her pleasure—saw him flush unexpectedly. Fulke was aware, in fact, that he had stumbled upon a boorish remark. His discomfiture made her feel that he must own a decent sensibility in addition to his superabundant cleverness. And what he had said hadn't really been so tactless, after all. Had he been eighteen, or thereabout, it would have been downright oafish. That he and she belonged to different generations (which was how she judged of their situation) rendered it no more than a kind of jocular and avuncular remark.

'You see,' Fulke went on, recovering himself, 'the basis of true love is that a man's mistress—I mean in the old-fashioned sense of the word—should be for quite some time up on a balcony or on the other side of a high wall.'

'Juliet,' Dora said, 'didn't stay that way for long.'

81

'No—and her story wasn't a happy one. She ought to have watched her step.'

'You mustn't be flippant to Dora about Juliet,' Penelope said. 'Dora was Juliet in our last year's school play.'

'And I wanted Penelope as my Romeo,' Dora struck in. 'But it was decided otherwise through some disgusting act of favouritism.'

'Is your annual play an all-girl affair, then?' Fulke asked. 'Surely I'm right in thinking there's a most reputable boys' school almost over your own high wall. Why don't you join up? You could do tremendous plays together. I'd turn up in the audience like a shot.'

'We're old-fashioned, as Penelope says. And our headmistress points out that Shakespeare's plays were originally one-sex affairs. Nothing but men and boys. So why not nothing but girls?'

'I think it a very poor argument.' Fulke said this with decision. 'What about this year's play?'

'Oh, things are looking up—although not in that direction. We're going to do *As You Like It*—only Shakespeare is regarded as really *safe*—and Penelope is going to be Rosalind. She'll be tiptop.'

'Certainly she will. And book me in for the third row of the stalls—if you run to stalls, that is.'

This time, it was Penelope who flushed. Fulke's response had ended with a vague joke, but this didn't detract from the air of spontaneous conviction with which it had begun. Penelope misdoubted her capacities as a Rosalind, who plainly hadn't been a clergyman's daughter. She would make, she believed, a better Isabella, or even Helena. But neither *Measure for Measure* nor *All's Well that Ends Well*—although undoubtedly by Shakespeare—would have been regarded as at all a suitable play. In this estimate of her own endowments Penelope may, of course, have been entirely mistaken. And however this may have been, she was already in a state of some alarm over what lay before her. She didn't doubt her capacity, although she may have doubted her inclination, to be a Head Girl. But the apex of Shakespearean comedy was another matter. So she became a shade withdrawn during the rest of the walk through the park. When they arrived at its boundary Fulke remarked that he hoped they might fix up something soon, and that meanwhile he would say good-bye. He refrained from the archaic courtesy of assisting the ladies over the stile. The girls failed to refrain, a minute or so later, from a backward glance. Fulke at a middle distance seemed more naked still. The little bathing-slip scarcely showed on his slim hips and compact bottom.

'What did you think of him?' Penelope asked as she and Dora neared the vicarage. 'Is he nice?'

'I don't at all know. He was fun about the plays. But that earlier bit about time and art and beauty was a bit odd. It wasn't exactly a showing-off, but more a buttering-up. Taking us for granted as thoughtful adults: something like that. But I can believe in him as a writer.'

'Why?'

'Well, I almost had a feeling he was automatically at work on us. Wondering about our possibilities—but not in the crude way you're sometimes aware of men doing that, imagining you with your clothes off, and so on. Perhaps seeing us as contrasting types that he might drop into a play or something.'

'I'm not at all sure he wasn't taking *your* clothes off, Dora. Right at the start.'

'Well, we had the advantage of him, in a way, since all *his* clothes were off already. And he does strip pretty.'

'What an awful expression!'

'We've taken to going in for rather awful talk, haven't we? As for being glanced over in the gross male way, I can't say I wasn't—if ever so briefly—aware of it. But it didn't terribly please me. Do you know what I thought he was thinking? "Oh, yes—but I've been there before." Something like that.'

'Dora, this is becoming quite horrible. Do you mean you felt yourself to be in the presence of—well, of a sated voluptuary?'

'That's an awful expression, too. I can't think, Penelope, where your reading has lain of late.'

'It's a very good and precise expression. But the question is whether it applies. Isn't it just that what I said about *roués* has put it in both our heads?'

'Very probably—and I don't want to traduce your neighbour Fulke Ferneydale. Probably he *is* very nice. But what I'm sure of is that he is a troubled young man. One can't remotely pin it down. But it does somehow come through.'

'It may be that he feels the sort of things he has written so far are not what he ought really to be after as an artist.'

'That would at least be a respectable explanation. But, now, here's something more important. Shall we really go and swim with him?'

'Yes, we will.' Penelope had answered on the instant. 'Just the three of us mayn't be exactly *comme il faut*. But I'll be chaperoning you and you'll be chaperoning me.'

VI

Caspar Ferneydale's visit to Paris ought to have given him considerable satisfaction. He loved the city, and at the age of twenty-six felt that it had been for many years familiar to him. He also felt that twenty-six was an unusually early age at which to have conferred on him even the small ceremonial rôle he had undertaken. The scholar who had died had been an eminent lay polemicist of the Faith, and a Tertiary of the same Order to which Caspar—again precociously—had been admitted in England. So Caspar had been appointed to attend a formal commemorative occasion in a respectable representative character. And this constituted too, he felt, one up to the journal he now edited. It was a journal, he would candidly have admitted, in need of anything of that sort that came along. Quarter by quarter, its appearance was not much remarked; it hung obstinately in the dusty rear of several older-established publications of similar kidney; there was danger that it would even fade away into the limbo of numerous fugitive ventures similarly regardless of popular appeal. But he would write for it an account of his mission, and of relevant aspects of the current French intellectual scene, sufficiently distinguished to mark him as something more than the importunate solicitor of unremunerative contributions from authentic but much preoccupied intellectuals of one kind and another. With luck his piece might particularly please that Old Catholic nobleman on whose modest munificence the continued existence of his journal largely depended.

But Caspar *was* only twenty-six, and around him (as once around his brother in an earlier season) Paris expanded itself in quite other directions. Was it not a vast and many-faceted engine of refined pleasures such as Fulke would have told him that Henry James or somebody had once described it? It was true that Fulke's first sampling of this had been merely gross—or in part gross and in part absurd. But Caspar felt that he himself harboured the capacity for other sensations, could he only grasp at that simple *joie de vivre* which, alas, seemed destined perpetually to elude him. So he moved from one familiar scene to another in an elegiac frame of mind.

He lacked, he told himself, even intellectual passion. He ought to have remained a don—he had really met with ill luck there—and developed on the one hand some compassable field of scholarly enquiry and on the other a gently fulfilled domesticity with wife and child among similarly disposed persons inhabiting the villas of North Oxford. At least he would be up to that—although here again, indeed, passion was an elusive endowment. Unlike Fulke—who was scurrying, he knew, in a restless way from mistress to mistress—he had remained depressingly ineffective as a sexual being. Yet he was a sexual being of the simplest sort, for whom the achieving of fulfilment in this very normal aspect of life ought itself to be simple. He remembered how that old donkey Henry Rich had asked him whether he had any thought of the priesthood, and how at the time he had evaded a direct answer. Actually, he could have given it at once. He didn't doubt—at least he thought he didn't doubt—his unswerving loyalty to Holy Church. But no more did he doubt his entire lack of any inclination to celibacy. He respected that particular act of dedication enormously, but at the same time he saw and feared its loneliness. Of course you couldn't be lonely—in a radical sense you couldn't be lonely—if you had given yourself wholly to Christ. The idea frightened him, all the same. It was unfortunate, he was sometimes capable of thinking, that the Anglican Church was deeply and hopelessly in heresy. Had it not been so, he might have made a contented (and rather more theologically active) Henry Rich in due season.

In Paris, however, there had still been (indeed, there increasingly were) significant doors at which he could with propriety and acceptance present himself. Nobody knew very much about him, but he was understood to be establishing himself in similar circles in his own country, and he was undoubtedly well-informed. That he also possessed a certain sharpness and subtlety of mind was known only to the few people who happened to have read some of his carefully prepared articles and reviews. There was little that was remarkable or in any way memorable about his conversation, and about his manner or bearing there was nothing, at least in strange company, except a common English upper-class diffidence unlikely to arrest any attention whatever. But at one party he persuaded an eminent Academician to write for his journal a short essay on the later, and edifying, career of Charles Péguy, at that time known in England, if at all, only as a poet with a dotty obsession with Joan of Arc. This was quite a *coup*, so that Caspar returned home well pleased with himself after all.

But just what 'home' meant to Caspar Ferneydale at this time, he might have found it difficult to say. It did, of course, mean England; and to his native soil in this sense he was notably attached. Although he did more reading in foreign languages than in his own, and was strongly attracted by at least certain aspects of French culture, and again even although his Church so majestically transcended all national boundaries, he nevertheless had little taste for anything to be called cosmopolitan life. In this he differed from his brother. Fulke liked to feel equally at home, or equally without any felt need to be at home, in whatever corner of the globe he had planted himself for a time. There were, in fact, the makings of an expatriate in Fulke, whereas Caspar was by instinct a home-keeping, or at least home-returning, youth. He might have told you that he lived in London— this on the strength of having secured himself a *pied-à-terre* loosely attached to a Catholic mission maintaining a tenuous existence in Bethnal Green. But he was at least at Mallows Hall less infrequently than Fulke, and might have spent even more time there had he not been conscious that his parents—or certainly his father—regarded him as a kind of family puzzle, or indeed problem, hanging around when he ought to be getting on. James Ferneydale made little of his elder son's literary productions, and was rendered at times uneasy by what he heard about his life. But there was no doubt that Fulke was beginning to make money; his habit of buying expensive motor-cars and the like without any call upon a family exchequer would alone have demonstrated this; and he even paid his parents a species of rent by the regular importation of Havana cigars and delicacies from Messrs Fortnum and Mason. Caspar's employments were equally incomprehensible, but his emoluments therefrom appeared nugatory, so that he lived on those slightly more than adequate hand-outs which prosperous and preoccupied business men get in the habit of dispensing to sons as a matter of course from quite an early age. Caspar himself found nothing positively uncomfortable about this.

But it was slightly discouraging, all the same, so that he was inclined to dwell upon the necessity of his being much in London were he adequately to keep his finger upon the intellectual pulse of the age.

On the present occasion, however, Caspar had taken it into his head that he must soon write not merely that choice piece upon his late small expedition but positively a substantial and deeply meditated book, upon which he would make a start by spending at least a couple of summer months quietly at Mallows. He had already prepared for this by sending down a large packing-case containing the primary materials for such a venture.

But first he paid a visit to Oxford, a little in the spirit of a John Henry Newman taking a peep at the paradise from which he had been expelled. Of course there had been no theological animus whatever in Caspar's failure to keep a permanent foothold there. After all, something like a Catholic High Command had long been comfortably established at Oxford, the prime duty of which was to maintain a thoughtful eye on all that was promising and unpromising in the behaviour alike of recent converts and of Cradle Cats. On Caspar himself Father Fisher still kept tabs, and it was primarily to report to this spiritual director that the visit was made.

Father Fisher was an influential man. It was even believed that his name did not pass unmentioned in Rome whenever the Curia chanced upon the problem of the evangelization of England. His austerity was also formidable, while being at the same time of that higher sort which accommodates itself to a graceful participation in the material comforts and recruitments proper in the entertaining of guests. He appeared to have plenty of leisure for Caspar, taking him to dine and spend the evening with the Jesuits at Campion Hall, and on the following day entertaining him to a simple midday meal which ran to an excellent claret. They then walked round Christ Church Meadow.

Oxford in the Long Vacation was already in those years not at all as it is described by Charles Lamb. The era of mass tourism had not arrived, but summer visitors were remarkably numerous, all the same. For some time adventurous Americans had again been going on holiday abroad, and had returned home to assure their compatriots that what they called 'conditions' in Europe were sufficiently restored to be tolerable to those of pioneering mind. So—for the most part in small parties—there were plenty of these around. Oddly contrasting with them were larger contingents of young people from the continent, roaming with packs on their backs a world that seemed to them suddenly of marvellous extension. All this had taken a decade to come about, and it had been a decade during which Oxford's factories for building motor-cars had been breeding banausic hordes not yet comfortably accommodated with shopping and recreative facilities in their own rapidly proliferating suburbs. This social mix-up troubled nobody, and indeed the period had already begun in which the undergraduates of the university had hit upon the wholesome idea of managing to dress (if not always to behave) in a manner identical with that of their contemporaries from the conveyor belts of Cowley.

But if the city had become a crowded and bustling place, Christ Church Meadow remained mysteriously inviolate. Here and there on its northern perimeter, where there were modest expanses of mown and unfenced grass, a few people came at midday to eat their sandwiches or venture upon more or less restrained approaches to making love. But the great open space running down to the river was peopled only by sheep or cattle, transported thither by Christ Church at some expense to impart a judicious air of rurality to the scene. There were atrocious persons bent upon constructing a high road across Christ Church Meadow, and the cattle represented one of the more obvious and publicly exhibited measures for frustrating anything of the sort. What remained curious was the fact that walking round Christ Church Meadow, which was the gentle exercise of half an hour, seemed to remain the habit of the same small number of meditative persons as had pursued it in the age of Matthew Arnold and Benjamin Jowett. Caspar Ferneydale and Father Fisher were in the enjoyment of this on the present afternoon.

'That was a delightful occasion last night,' Caspar said politely. 'But it gives me something to confess. Those young men attending upon us, and so arduously beginning at the bottom of a ladder, made me feel something of an outsider still. That sort of discipline I couldn't begin on now.'

'No, you could not.' Father Fisher invariably concurred at once in evident truths, and he knew that Caspar was no more likely to become a Jesuit than he was to become a member of the Papal Guard in habiliments designed by Michelangelo for the purpose. 'And what you say has often been said to me by converts. Strange garments, you know, cleave not to their mould but with the aid of use.'

'That's certainly true.' In point of fact, Caspar didn't care to have his Catholicism described as still a strange garment. It had now sat upon him for a good many years, and he remembered with distaste the uneasy period in which he had made a habit of 'reconsidering his position' every six months or so. In the past twenty-four hours Father Fisher had been the soul of tact in a pastoral way. He had discussed Caspar's projected book in a detailed and penetrating manner, and always with the implication that it was as certain to be influential as it was to be achieved within at least a short space of years. Intelligent and widely-read laymen had their use; indeed, they were extremely important. But Father Fisher was probably relieved that Caspar Ferneydale was not Fulke Ferneydale, upon whose opinions and activities he had evidently taken the trouble to inform himself fairly fully. Nothing was more tricky than a convert, free of the stricter disciplines of the Church and possessed of a strong creative flair. There were several prominent novelists like that in England, and probably playwrights too, and it didn't help when they went a little off the rails. Caspar Ferneydale was in a simpler category. What was important was that he should be confirmed and fortified in a sober understanding of his rightful and most acceptable rôle in whatever struggle lay ahead.

But Father Fisher wasn't a man to hurry things. He was aware, too, that despite all his care what was in his mind was unlikely to be wholly concealed from Caspar's, in which he knew there lay a good deal of intuitive alertness as well as valuable intellectual ability. So now he talked at some length, and with much practical sagacity, about his protégé's immediate problems as an editor. It was only when the two men had sat down on a bench commanding a view of the placid Isis and the line of deserted college barges that he approached other matters.

'The going is likely to be tough,' Father Fisher said. 'And this time I make the remark in terms of the largest perspectives.'

'It always is, isn't it? The battle goes on for ever.'

'Yes, indeed, Caspar. And we must be temperate in our talk of a new Dark Age. Through the centuries it has been a facile road to turning glum—and there's nothing more absurd, you know, than a glum Christian. Still, one has to look ahead. Horrors have happened often enough, and some of the most remarkable have occurred within the orbit of the Church. The rationalist view of us as among the villains of the piece can undoubtedly find its evidences here and there. But even the most dreadful aberrations of heresy-hunting and the like have usually been more or less local phenomena. What seems now to lie ahead is a proliferation of evil on a world-wide scale. Everywhere acquisitiveness and the rage for material things may drive men to torment and destroy one another on a scale almost unexampled in the past.'

'So what are we to do, Father?'

'Find each his appointed station, I suppose, within which to play his part. The priesthood for some of us, the gaining of a beneficent authority in public affairs or the intellectual or literary sphere for others. And we must all gather strength and equilibrium as we best may. I hold it to be true that for the majority of men, however varying their temperaments and abilities, these qualities are most securely sustained and nourished upon a basis of the domestic sanctities.'

'Are you telling me, Father, that I ought to get married—and to a woman who will back me up?'

'My dear boy; not quite that.' Father Fisher was pleased by this directness on Caspar's part. There was a good deal of native evasiveness about the young man, and a liking for making his points obliquely. So here was at once a token of the priest's skill in fostering a relationship of confidence over intimate matters, and a warning that such authority was to be exercised warily. 'No, not quite that,' he repeated. 'There are those who give such advice baldly to young men who have been drawn into leading irregular lives. But even in such cases I am myself inclined to consider it as in danger of being rash and presumptuous. Yet I confess that I am suggesting to you a considera-tion to which your private thoughts should be given.'

Caspar accepted this in silence, judging that Father Fisher's turn of phrase had indicated his sense that this delicate subject should not be touched on further for the moment. And Father Fisher confirmed the accuracy of the conjecture by presently remarking on the curious fact that the barges, although individually lacking elegance, were yet delightful in their total effect. Caspar responded as he could, his 'private thoughts' having been cast into considerable confusion. On the one hand he felt faintly demoted by what had been said. But on the other his respect for Father Fisher's counsels was increased—and not least from their underlying suggestion that in such matters one ought not to hurry along. For some months he must give himself time to reflect. Or—for that matter—some years.

But a couple of hours brought him back to Mallows, and also, somewhat to his surprise, into the company of his brother. About Fulke there was no sense, as there commonly was, of his having dropped in for a week. He had made, it appeared, a very recent change in his plans for the summer, and was establishing working quarters of a sort in the two or three rooms always kept available for him. He had a good deal to say—in fact he was quite unusually communicative—about his current literary preoccupations. The plays had been all very well, and it was scarcely unimportant that they were still making pots of money. But a certain stigma indefinably attached to that sort of precocious success. Further affairs of the same kind might see him fatally typed as a purveyor of froth and bubble. Quite apart from reputation, moreover, he felt that such productions left him short of space and air. It wasn't for nothing that the novel was so clearly becoming the predominant literary form of the age; it was rather that the complexities of that age, the seriousness of its problems for anybody who had the instinct for seriousness in him at all, called for a medium there was room to turn round in; and to get hooked on the theatre was virtually to abandon that. And although novels were in a sense two a penny, and for the most part reviewed in batches by acrid women, they were less than plays at the mercy of the sheep-like propensities of run-of-the-mill critics.

'Is it really as bad as that?' Caspar asked.

'It's just like that. As a playwright you can be living at the Ritz one week—supposing you have any such inclination—and the next week find yourself in a bed-sit as the proprietor of little more than a suitcase. It just so happens that my plays have had the bastards nearly all clapping their little trotters like mad. Not that a few of them didn't say pretty filthy things.'

'I'm sorry to hear it.' In this last remark of his brother's there had lurked a tone which didn't so much surprise Caspar as remind him of what in recent years he had come to see clearly enough. And literally to see, at times: a dark flush of sudden uncontrolled resentment that spoke of something deep—and surely far from attractive—in Fulke's nature. Fulke could be quite desperately vulnerable to slights. One could even suspect that he registered them, docketed them, for a stored up vengeance one day. It was an unexpected facet of personality in one who took so much carelessly and in his stride.

'Yes,' he heard Fulke now reiterating. 'Take to the theatre for your living, and it may be indecent luxury one day—demeaning jet-set stuff and being hauled round parties as a celebrity—and something uncomfortably like the dole queue the next.'

Caspar listened to this circular talk—a characteristic shilly-shally, he judged it, between the market-place and something at least of nobler intention—with what sympathy he could. He genuinely wanted his brother to raise his sights, to trade up. Let Fulke be James Joyce, if he could manage it, and he himself would be perfectly happy as Stanislaus. But he had various doubts about it. The radical doubt, of course, concerned the true reach of Fulke's endowments. But he also doubted, as being a legend of the romantic decadence, the salubrity, for a major artist, of Bohemian ways and Bohemian harassments. On his more intimate life, too, Fulke was not wholly uncommunicative, and Caspar had arrived at a fairly clear view of an odd sort of desperation attending his brother's conduct of it. There was something messy about all those women, none of whom Caspar had ever set eyes on. Not that Caspar wasn't also envious of such facile fornication—and almost certainly adultery, too, for that matter. He wondered at times whether he could set Father Fisher successfully to work on Fulke. It didn't seem at all a hopeful idea.

There was also a kind of awkwardness in two utterly diverse literary aspirations proceeding cheek by jowl beneath one substantially isolated and distinctly philistine roof. Two typewriters tapping away at decidedly different tempos! Caspar had no doubt that his brother, once launched on the long novel which appeared to be on his mind, would proceed in a kind of *furor scribendi* for weeks on end, while the pace of his own philosophical perpendings would be to this as the tortoise's to the hare's. It was even faintly ludicrous, like the rival family scribblings of the Brontës in their awful parsonage. Would each read to the other what he had written during the day? Nonsensical

93

thoughts of this kind almost prompted Caspar to pack up his books and periodicals again, and retreat, even in August, to his small oven of a room in Bethnal Green.

In fact, from the first the brothers got on quite well. Perhaps three or four years earlier than the thought commonly comes to young men, Fulke had arrived at the idea that he was a young man no longer, and that it was incumbent upon him to take measures to keep fit. Caspar found this curious, and a notion which any observer might have judged more likely to incubate in his own, Caspar's, head. Perhaps it had something to do with standards of sexual athleticism into which it would be indecent to inquire. However that might be, Fulke insisted on a good deal of tennis. They were still reasonably well matched, and still perhaps exhibited those temperamental differences in play upon which the Reverend Henry Rich had sagely commented almost a decade before.

'And you've turned up,' Fulke said on the second day, 'just in time for my water party. It's uncommonly useful, because you'll balance it up. I suppose you possess some bathers?'

'Just what are you talking about?'

'It began with the vicarage girl—Penelope, you know. She has a friend called Dora Something-or-other staying with her until the end of the month. Quite a piece, Dora, in a juvenile way. So I've asked them both to come and swim in the lake on Thursday afternoon.'

'How very odd! And also Penelope's papa?'

'Lord, no. Old Rich had a kind of stroke, you remember, a few years ago, and Hurcomb made him go and swim regularly for therapeutic purposes in some horrible public baths. It turned Rich hydrophobic for life. But I'd not have asked him in any case. My water party's a young people's water party. At first I meant it to be just the two schoolgirls and myself, because I thought it might be amusing like that.'

'Have you taken to going in for them young, Fulke?'

'Not particularly, Cass.' Fulke frowned momentarily. He disliked his naturally inhibited brother trying to play up to him in this way. 'But I found Mother feeling that something more populous would be more decorous. So I've asked Hurcomb's new assistant, Charles Gaston, whom you haven't met. An Oxford man, and all that—

although at some obscure college or other. But livelier than some young medics tend to be.'

'And have you asked anybody else?'

'Sophie Dix—whom you might call the other girl next door. That's why you balance it up. And Mother is going to send down a picnic tea.'

'I still think it uncommonly odd. And I'm suspicious of that casual dropping in of Sophie Dix. A squire's daughter, and all that. But isn't she rather thick?'

'Anatomically, here and there, I'd say yes. And I just want to see her great breasts bulging on the brine.'

'Don't be so disgusting, Fulke. There are limits, after all.'

"But that's one of your favourite poets, Cass! Hardy in *The Dynasts*. Don't you remember? There are chaps who cry out, "A mermaid 'tis!" Actually, it's the captain's woman. The captain of a man o' war was free to cart a woman around with him in Napoleonic times.'

'I believe you've organized this whole load of rubbish simply because you have designs on this bulging young woman.' Caspar knew he had deliberately repeated the phrase because it offended him. There was something close to the dead common, surely, in slapping it out—whether from Thomas Hardy or not—about a woman whom one had invited to be one's guest in a few days' time.

'Designs?' Fulke said cheerfully. 'Oh, very probably. But you'll come?'

'Yes, I'll come.' Caspar said this without any irritating pretence of resignation. He had reservations about Sophie Dix; and about the schoolgirl called Dora he knew nothing at all. But he had a distinct feeling that he liked Penelope Rich.

95

VII

Six young people having a swim is not with any great appositeness to be called a 'water party', since the term suggests something more like a stately progress of gilded barges to the music of viols. So Fulke's use of it must have been mildly ironic, employed to distance a project he had initiated on impulse and was now dubious about. What had put it into his head? One of the three girls who were coming? Or all of the three girls who were coming? He didn't really know; wasn't at all sure that it hadn't the air of a kids' outing with plenty of toy balloons and ice-cream. Sophie Dix, although so abounding in the flesh, couldn't be much older than Penelope Rich and her friend. If he had designs on her in the manner Caspar had suggested, they certainly weren't old-established. The Ferneydales had never much bothered with the Dixes, and he didn't even know if their daughter was now formally regarded as grown up. The third young man, Charles Gaston, must be about Fulke's own age, and Fulke had taken to him at a recent meeting seemingly because he had talked intelligently about a few current books. To ask him to come swimming had perhaps been a little out of the way. Fulke had done so before even knowing whether the chap could swim—let alone have any list for doing so in a glorified duck-pond. An invitation to a tennis party would have been rather more in order.

Perhaps because of all this, Fulke took a good deal of trouble over his venture—to the surprise of Caspar, who didn't often see his brother much concerning himself with any recreative activities of a sort sanctioned in the Mallows world. Fulke had a tent put up for the girls, and provided it with this and that which he thought might be useful to them. There being not much shade near the lake, he had an awning to picnic under should the afternoon prove uncomfortably hot. He even rescued an abandoned canoe and had it scrubbed out and given a lick of varnish by a misdoubting gardener, perhaps feeling that this might bring 'water party' a little more into the picture. Observing the unexpected to-do, Caspar said that it was sure to rain, so that the party would become a watery one in an unwelcome sense. Fulke replied cheerfully that, in this event, they would all go indoors and play billiards—or ping-pong should the girls disclaim knowing one end of a billiard cue from the other. There was plenty of room in the Hall for any sort of high jinks they had a mind to.

In fact it proved to be a perfect day. Gaston turned up first, in shorts and with a towel swathed lightly round his neck. He might have been on the way, Caspar thought, from his obscure Oxford college to the river, there to take part in the galley-slave exercises dear to undergraduates of the heartier and more bone-headed sort. But to Caspar's astonishment he referred, as soon as he had been introduced, to a review Caspar had recently contributed to a journal quite as dry as his own. So there must be a little more to Charles Gaston than driving round the district scribbling useless prescriptions for old women. Gaston had by no means wholly approved of the review (the book · prompting which he seemed also to have read), and he explained why—briskly and cordially—in the course of five minutes' chat. Fulke was amused by this, but Caspar himself liked it. To have been noticed by anybody on anything he had anywhere propounded was still something grateful to him at all times.

The three young women arrived together, and it was evident that Miss Dix was already known to her companions. Fulke received them with the gaiety proper in a host who has organized a chancy affair, even greeting Dora as Juliet and Penelope as Ganymede—which puzzled her until she remembered that it was under this name that she was destined to pass through a good deal of *As You Like It*. It clearly pleased him to show that he remembered their previous conversation about theatrical activities. About Sophie Dix he seemed to have nothing to recall, but made up for this by briefly turning on a marked moment of gratifying admiration. With Fulke in this mood everything looked tolerably promising—even the pool itself, which he had caused to be skimmed of its more obtrusive vegetable components.

The elder Ferneydales had refrained from coming down to keep an eye on the scene. Even the tea-picnic was to be transported to the site by a parlourmaid. When that happened the occasion would take on quite the air of a youthful *fête-champêtre*. But first everybody had to disrobe. Gaston chucked his towel on the grass, slipped off his T-shirt, zipped down his shorts, and was ready for action at once, his bathing-trunks being already *in situ*. The Ferneydales, having rather more to dispose of, went into the hut. The girls, correspondingly, retired to the tent, and took a little longer to emerge. When they did so, a distinction was to be observed between them. Penelope and her friend were in what might still have been called bathing-costumes: well removed, indeed, from the drab affairs probably standard at their school, but nevertheless clothing the greater part of their persons. Sophie wore a bikini, the two parts of which didn't markedly differ in hue from Sophie's own pelt, which might have been described as pleasingly honey-coloured rather than pink or pinko-grey.

'*C'est ravissant, cela,*' Fulke murmured to his brother. '*Un anéantissement de la surface vêtue; une minimisation extrême de la pudeur.*'

Caspar might have replied, 'A kind of vulgarization of Renoir,' if he hadn't been thoroughly annoyed. To be thus speaking in an undertone about a guest was surely the height of bad form—or, rather, the abysmal depth of it—and it signalled the possibility that Fulke might be in the mood to perpetrate some freakish outrage at any time. But nothing of the sort occurred. Fulke's behaviour was impeccable and gay. He sang out *Eenee, meenee, mainee, mo* by way of determining who should dive in first, and improvised competitive events in a suitably casual manner. Above all, he had no appearance of keeping an eye on anybody, or of justifying that former impression of Dora Quillinan's that he had the habit of wondering how he might drop you into a future work of fiction. Caspar, to whom he still talked occasional nonsense about creative writing and experimental psychology, was at least reassured that no experiment was being set up.

But if the bathing was a success it was probably because it didn't go on too long, climaxing in a kind of water polo sufficiently boisterous to stir up more mud than was agreeable at least to the girls. So they all returned to dry land, and found that Fulke had provided tubs of clear water to sponge down from. The picnic arrived while they were getting dressed.

Penelope, whose decision to accept Fulke's proposal for swimming together had precipitated the whole affair, found that she had enjoyed it very much, including the virtual romp at the end. She didn't even greatly mind when Fulke, who was (perhaps significantly) a keen photographer, insisted on their all posing for him in turn in their wet and dishevelled state. Nevertheless, she was relieved when they had all become young ladies and gentlemen again, properly habited and sipping their China tea. The ethos of the vicarage still went round with Penelope quite a lot, and she felt glad that it hadn't occurred to her father to stroll into the park and observe the scene. He would have been aware that young people, male and female together, engage in such activities—at least if decently bred—without any disabling self-consciousness of a sexual sort—or at least with an entire masking of anything of the kind. But he would certainly have judged Sophie Dix to be 'fast'. In fact Penelope doubted her being anything of the kind. She was merely rather stupid, and had believed her indecorous costume to be figuratively as well as actually in the swim. Of Charles Gaston Mr Rich would certainly have approved, since he believed that cultivated persons in the minor professions (such as the medical) were becoming noticeably rare. And in Dora's comportment he would have found nothing to qualify his approbation of a future ambassador's daughter. The young Ferneydales were a little different. Her father regarded Caspar with some respect, as a serious person who had unfortunately fallen into grievous doctrinal error. But of Fulke he seemed to have heard things that he didn't like at all. It was probable that, on balance, he would have been rendered uneasy by this slightly odd occasion.

Caspar's conversation at tea was addressed at first to Penelope. Perhaps not very appropriately, he began telling her about his projected book.

'Of course it's miles away,' he said, 'from Fulke's sort of thing. I couldn't write plays, or any sort of fiction, for toffee.'

'Would you like to?' Penelope asked. 'It seems that a lot of people are anxious to become authors.'

'Well, I suppose I am anxious to be *that*. But "authorship" can be made to cover a good deal, you know. Kant or Spinoza could be called an author. Or, for that matter, St Catherine of Siena, although it would sound a bit rum.'

To Penelope these were merely names—but names, she knew, slightly surprising as turning up after water polo. So she said nothing, but looked at Caspar with the grave attention she felt to be appropriate. This encouraged him.

'Not that I'll be steering altogether clear of imaginative writing. The archetypal myths I want to deal with often live on, you see, in unlikely places. Even, conceivably, in one of Fulke's amusing plays, although without his being conscious of the fact. It's a testament to their vitality. And that vitality derives—and this will be my grand point—from their relationship, again often hard to discern, to the central myth of all: the one that comes to us in the Western World under the colours of Christian dogma.'

Naturally enough, this again held Penelope silent. It might even have had this effect on Father Fisher, had it happened that he too had been playing water polo. It is unlikely that the distinctly disturbing word 'colours' had escaped Caspar as yet when discussing his projected *opus magnum* with his spiritual director. Penelope could see only that Caspar was serious and truthful, but had got her age a little wrong, and consequently her present intellectual horizons. She was pleased, all the same. It was her ambition to take a thoughtful and sober view of life, which she had already discovered to be a vastly mysterious affair, and one unquestionably daunting to look at squarely. Perhaps the grand test consisted precisely in being able to do that. And whoever Kant and Spinoza had been, it was evident that Caspar (decidedly unlike his brother) was of one mind with her here. It had been a philosopher who, distinguishably a shade conscientiously, had been punching a rubber ball around the Ferneydales' bathing place. But it also appeared evident to her that it was without conscientious effort that Caspar's glance turned every now and then to the ample, and at the moment recumbent, form of Sophie Dix. Because Penelope enjoyed looking at picture books illustrating the history of art, there even came fleetingly into her head the dim image of a painting of Titian's called something like *Sacred and Profane Love*. She didn't in the least see herself as Sacred, but felt that Sophie could stand in as Profane very well.

If her own glance occasionally turned away from the earnestly discoursing young philosopher, it was in the direction of his brother. Fulke had so far not talked to her very much, and she was a little piqued by this. But at least neither was he talking to either of the other girls, who were at present engaged in some not very lively discussion of their own. He was conversing with Charles Gaston, if that could be called conversation when two men were sprawled side by side on their backs and gazing at the sky. But they did, thus disposed, seem to invite comparison. Dr Hurcomb's new assistant hadn't bothered to put on more than his shorts, which a little detached him from the now predominant tea-party aspect of the situation. What he presented to the still scarcely westering sun was a chest displaying small dark nipples with a light dusting of golden hair descending from between them to a tummy conventionally to be described as flat as a board. Fulke, on the other hand, was no longer on view as a torso, since he had resumed a fully clothed condition. But then Penelope had already been favoured with a leisured look at his physique, and she had to conclude that neither young man held any advantage over the other in this literally superficial regard.

But what did their features as indexes of character respectively reveal? She decided that they didn't here much resemble one another. Gaston was probably by a few years the younger. Fulke's features in full sunshine, and even in the sort of drowsy repose at present possessing them, suggested things that Gaston's didn't. Perhaps it was what people called the impress of experience. There were those little lines round the eyes. There was even a hint that at the temples his hair might be turning prematurely grey. And one could feel, too, that at any moment an unexpected motility, expressive perhaps of enjoyment or suffering, might overtake what were at the moment those contented and slightly parted lips. Gaston's features told one less. But what they did somehow seem to speak of was a strong and settled mind. He was what they called a well-balanced man. If one thought in terms of a life's journey with one or the other, Gaston might have the edge on Fulke at the humdrum level of reliability and stability.

These were perceptions and imaginings drawing the mind away from what the mere eye perceives. Indeed, if Penelope at this time found herself quite frequently thinking in particular about Fulke, it wasn't, she suspected, much on the score of that immediate physical attraction which she and Dora had recently so sagely discussed. It was rather because Fulke was famous: the sole person of her acquaintance so far whom the world could be said to have heard of. So even a glance from him was flattering.

Confronting this picture of the matter, Penelope was disposed to accord herself a good mark for candid self-scrutiny. And she continued to glance across at Fulke from time to time, even while equally continuing to listen respectfully to Caspar's sketch of his present intellectual position. Then a slight change in the configuration of the party took place. Charles Gaston, through sheer soaking in sunshine it may have been, appeared actually to have fallen asleep. Fulke was continuing to offer desultory remarks to the heavens. But presently, as if becoming aware that their only response was silence, he sat up and glanced down at his supine companion. He did this, it seemed to Penelope, with a curious intentness of regard—rather as if fearful that Gaston had fainted, or even departed this life with a highly dramatic abruptness. Then Fulke got swiftly to his feet, and with no further glance at the sleeping man walked over to join Dora and Sophie.

Fulke Ferneydale was touchy, Penelope thought, and had resented even his occasional remarks having assumed the function of a lullaby. And now she found that Caspar, too, had observed the incident—deep in speculative considerations though he had been.

'I say!' he said. 'Fulke must have been boring that chap Gaston. Chattering to him about actresses, probably, and that sort of thing. And now Gaston's woken up, and may be feeling himself rather abruptly deserted. Do you think I ought to go over and have a word with him myself?'

'Yes, I do. I'll join the others.'

'As a matter of fact, Gaston is remarkably well-informed on some matters I've lately been thinking about quite a lot.'

'Unlike me, Caspar.'

'Penelope, I didn't mean——' Caspar broke off, quite surprisingly upset. 'You see, I love talking to you,' he said. 'Even if it's just my own stupid stuff, and you're simply being polite about it.'

And before Penelope could frame any reply to this startling speech, Caspar Ferneydale had got up and hurried away.

In fact it took Penelope a minute or two to pull herself together and join Fulke and the other girls. Fulke appeared to have got round to teasing them about something she didn't at first catch on to, but this in a properly good-natured way.

'But you're going to enjoy Somerville very much, Dora,' she heard him say—and it was evident that he would now regard 'Miss Quillinan' as an unfriendly and formal manner of address. 'It won't be any sort of cloister, I agree. But you'll have plenty of time to work like mad if you want to. And even the butterflies and socialites—if there are such females there any longer—will concur with your tutors in forming a high opinion of your deserts. It's my guess that you'll become Head Girl there too. As will Penelope, for that matter.' Fulke was now aware of Penelope as having joined the group. 'If, that's to say, she decides to follow you along.'

'Do you advise me to?' Penelope asked—and discovered as she spoke quite a strong impulse to challenge Fulke from time to time. 'If they at all thought of having me, that is.'

'It's a hard question,' Fulke said humorously. 'As a matter of fact, it's a general conundrum I was having some chat with Charles Gaston about.'

'Until he went to sleep on you?' Dora asked suddenly. She seemed to have the same instinct to challenge Fulke as Penelope had. 'We were just noticing that.'

'Charles is earnest, I assure you, as well as somnolent. And he believes in looking ahead. Sophie, do you believe in looking ahead? Or do you stick to looking hopefully around you?'

This piece of mischief appeared to puzzle rather than offend Miss Dix, who actually swept the horizon briefly by way of reply. Sophie, Penelope thought, might be a socialite but couldn't very well be called a butterfly, being distinctly on too robust a scale for any such comparison.

'Careers,' Fulke said, having received only silence. 'Charles believes in careers. He says that if girls go to Oxford it should be to read Physiology and then Medicine. He says that women make better doctors than barristers—and that school-teaching is unthinkable, and the Army won't have them except as curiosities.'

'Does he regard marriage as a career?' Dora asked.

'We didn't get round to that. Certainly I do. But one doesn't have to go to Oxford in search of matrimony.'

'Are there any statistics?' Penelope asked. She had lately become aware of statistics as a mystery that in numerous fields increasingly commanded masculine attention. 'On what does most frequently happen, I mean, to women who go to universities.'

'They become secretaries.'

'And sit typing things?' Sophie asked. 'I think that sounds quite horrid.'

'Well, not exactly sitting in pools—as we've been doing this afternoon.' It amused Fulke to produce mild incomprehension in Sophie Dix. 'But they do follow up their Old French Philology or whatever with crash courses in that region. Big Business bosses—tycoons, as they now say—like to feel they have that sort of girl taking down their thoughts on scratch-pads just as they'd formerly taken down the pronouncements of Regius Professors and such like cattle in their lectures. They maintain, you see, that in important concerns like theirs a high value attaches to what they call trained minds—meaning some rather old-fashioned liberal education. But it's at bottom a matter of social prestige. "I'm interested to hear that your daughter's at Girton," they say. "My secretary was a Girton girl."'

'How very dismal!' Dora spoke as one having no doubt about this.

'Yes, indeed. Of course they do quite rationally need somebody guarding their door and answering their telephone who takes upper-class social relations more in her stride than perhaps they've been wholly bred up to themselves. But what has Oxford or Cambridge to do with that? Increasingly near to nothing at all. And the old-established chaps—the merchant-bankers and so forth—know it perfectly well. They like fillies out of their own stable on the whole—just as a matter of social ease, really. But they don't give a hoot for degrees in Modern History or PPE. That's why the gentry on whose fringes we respectfully move—the third baronets and the knights of the shires—tend increasingly to shove their surplus daughters straight into secretarial colleges.'

Miss Dix continued to look bewildered, but this time a little offended too. 'Fringes' (which in any case was markedly inaccurate) seemed to her a highly derogatory word. Dora looked as if she might fire up a little on the broader ground of feminism in general. But Penelope felt that she was in the presence of worldly wisdom, even if there was a hint in it of persuasions none too graciously expressed.

'Do you have a secretary, Fulke?' she asked. 'And a door she has to sit like a dragon before?'

'I had a siren for a time. But it didn't do.' Fulke, as sometimes happened with him, immediately looked as if he regretted this remark. 'I get along very well on my own,' he added. 'There's a chap called a theatrical agent who does this and that for me. And I'm not very constantly in demand, anyway. Particularly when I've got away from London, which I'm now intending to do for some time. I do occasionally think that, for a writer, there's a lot to be said for having some small lurking place abroad. And I even have something on the horizon, as a matter of fact. It's a very modest villa in France.'

Despite herself, Penelope was impressed by this suggestion of precocious affluence. She knew that one ought not to have too much regard for worldly things. But to be coming to command them through gifts of the imagination was surely a quality not to be despised. And her glance went once more from Fulke to his new acquaintance, Charles Gaston. Before Gaston, it was to be supposed, lay nothing more than an obscure if beneficent career as a country GP. So she was entitled to regard Fulke at least as the more interesting of these two young men. But yet again she felt—although without at all knowing why—that there was something unsatisfying in this conclusion.

Part Three

VIII

'WHO AMBLES TIME withal?' Dora Quillinan asked in a tone of idle reminiscence. Dora was paying one of her visits to the vicarage. 'Everybody seems to stay put at Mallows. It's one of its charms. Does anybody new ever arrive—or anybody familiar ever go away?'

'Dr Gaston—whom you probably remember—went away. He put in a spell on some sort of research in America. But admittedly he's back again now.'

'A rambler rather than an ambler.'

'I suppose it's my father with whom time may be said to amble. Although he can't be called a priest that lacks Latin.' Penelope could still recall Rosalind's exchanges with Orlando, although not only school but also Oxford was now behind her. 'He potters at his book. But his mind is turning a bit hazy, as you must have observed.'

'So that he feels it, and it worries him?'

'I don't think so—or not a great deal. Caspar, who has all the good intentions in the world, sometimes gets him fidgety by trying to talk philosophy with him. He wants to create a feeling of their being on easy and equal terms about that sort of thing. But of course Daddy doesn't keep up as Caspar does, and he doesn't like admitting that he's at sea. Caspar says there's a certain irony in the particular aberrations that occasionally overtake him. Daddy's book is to be about Time, you'll remember: a kind of serious version of that silly dialogue in Shakespeare's play. But what has happened to my father is that he keeps getting his own timing wrong. Sometimes it's comical and sometimes it's embarrassing. It was quite splendidly both last Sunday.' As she said this, Penelope's face lit up with mischief—which was something, Dora reflected, that it did less frequently than of old. 'It was in his sermon.'

'You don't mean that he went on and on for hours?'

'No, I don't. Nor that he began it all over again as soon as he'd finished it. Perhaps that lies in the future. The Future, incidentally, troubles Daddy a good deal. He says it's more baffling than the Past, which you can at least see diminishing in the distance. But where does the Future come from? He admits he hasn't a clue.'

'I call that very sensible of your father, Penelope. But tell me about last Sunday.'

'He simply got into the pulpit for his sermon, and began as he usually does. He said, 'In the name of the Father, and of the Son, and of the Holy Ghost—Amen.' Then he crossed himself—and suddenly remembered something he'd forgotten to announce a few minutes before. So he said, "Through. the customary kindness of Mr Ferneydale, the water-spaniel trials will take place in Mallows Park at two o'clock on Saturday afternoon". Then he went on to announce his text. It happened to be the bit about the dogs getting the crumbs that fall from the Master's table. Of course nobody laughed—not even the unfortunate children who are made to turn up and serve as a choir. I suppose they didn't see the fun.'

Dora saw the fun—and found herself wondering what else she was coming to see during these occasional visits to Mr Rich's home. Decidedly not yet among them was how Penelope had come to marry Caspar Ferneydale. She'd have been much less surprised had her friend married Fulke—although the result of that might have been disastrous as the achieved marriage was not. Caspar was undoubtedly a devoted and affectionate husband, and perhaps it didn't at all matter that he hadn't much got on. Nobody who much gets on is likely to settle down to domesticity in his father-in-law's abode. And here the oddity was emphasized by Caspar's own native ground being no farther off than over a stile or through a gate. Presumably the need to keep an eye on the increasingly eccentric Henry Rich was a factor in the arrangement, and Dora knew that there had been a certain amount of housekeeping chaos in the vicarage when Mrs Gibbins had suddenly dropped dead over her ancient kitchen stove. But only a temporary accommodation might have been expected to succeed upon that. Had the sole alternative appealing to Caspar been to maintain his bride under his own ample parental roof, and had Penelope dug in her heels against this? Dora had never ventured to inquire.

Financial considerations might have been involved. Caspar's species of literary production plainly didn't earn a bean, and every now and then there were rumours that the Ferneydale business concerns weren't doing too well. Fulke Ferneydale must now, of course, be a rich rather than a merely prosperous man. But that would be beside the point, since it was unthinkable that Penelope would consent to being consistently helped out by a brother-in-law. And Fulke, for that matter, appeared to be wholly divorced from his family, his private life belonging to the same region of vague rumour as his father's standing with his bank. What Dora did know was that Fulke was somewhere rather firmly lodged in a secret corner of Penelope's mind.

Time ambles with others as well as philosophically insufficient clergymen. Did it a little amble, Dora wondered, with Penelope herself, oddly functioning as the lady of the vicarage while married to a papist doggedly speculative in print whenever he could command it? There had, Dora knew, been of necessity an undertaking that Caspar's children would be brought up in the Catholic faith, and it had been much to old Mr Rich's credit that his ecumenical sense had prompted him to concur in this. So far—and it was now a matter of several years—no children had appeared. Penelope was silent about the fact. But Dora herself—who was so decidedly attractive a young woman—remained unmarried, and there had been no talk about that either. The marriage they had a little talked about—because it had been so unexpected—was Fulke's. And Dora was suddenly prompted to turn to this topic now. The two young women were in the vicarage garden, and there was nobody in sight except (as once before) Tommy. But Tommy Elbrow was now a sturdy young man, with behind him a spell in the army which had a little broadened his horizons, but now back at Mallows, fully in charge of his former domain, and with a recently acquired wife and child of his own.

'Time didn't amble with your brother-in-law,' Dora said. 'I mean in the matrimonial way. Do you think that—to put it vulgarly—it was a shot-gun affair? Who wrote a novel called *The Amazing Marriage?*'

'Meredith.' Penelope had ended up by reading English at Oxford.

'It was certainly that. That perfectly awful girl!' Dora noted that an unexpected shadow had fallen over Penelope's face. 'You don't mind my saying that about a relation of yours by marriage?'

'Of course not. But I think you are unjust to Sophie. She isn't clever, and it was never evident that she tried to mitigate the fact by any devotion to serious pursuits.' It was as if Penelope was producing this piece of vicarage primness to give herself time to think. 'It's only that chief disparity between Fulke and herself that makes the marriage seem remarkable. And unpromising, too, no doubt. But sexually she was, and I suppose still is, very appealing indeed.'

'Bitches with *that* must have been two-a-penny with Fulke. Why *marry* one?'

'Sophie Dix may have held out. She was brought up with very conventional ideas, after all. And it does seem that a man can get so besotted with a woman that he'll stand before an altar with her and say those tremendous things just to be able to tumble her into bed.'

'Marry in haste and repent at leisure. But I'd hardly think of Fulke as that sort of man.' Dora was beginning to regret the turn this conversation had taken. One odd Ferneydale marriage was bound to have as a shadowy context another one. 'Of course,' she went on, feeling she mustn't abruptly shut up on it, 'there's coming to be more and more divorce blowing around, and legally and technically it's going to be easier and easier. I read somewhere the other day that, if present trends continue, one marriage in three will be breaking up by the 1980s. And whether or not there are any children by it. That would be a factor, wouldn't it, with your brother-in-law?'

'I suppose Fulke has children.'

Dora Quillinan found herself sitting down abruptly on a rustic bench, and with a sense that she had stumbled on something almost pathological. Penelope couldn't have spoken out of absolute ignorance. She had simply allowed to get a shade out-of-hand an attitude she had adopted towards Fulke Ferneydale and his affairs in general.

'Sophie had a son almost straight away,' Dora replied gently. 'That's why I said that stupid thing about a shot-gun marriage.'

'I'm wool-gathering. It must be the sight of Tommy, that ancient flame. *He* has a son called Damian. A queer sort of name to penetrate to the folk.'

'Yes, isn't it?' Dora's discomfort had grown in face of Penelope's random remark. She had a sense, too, that some sort of revelation was coming along. 'Fulke made rather an out-of-the-way choice of name for his son, too,' she said. 'Silvan.'

'Yes.' Penelope seemed to have forgotten her momentary profession of ignorance. 'Silvan Ferneydale. It was certainly laying it on a bit thick in the rural way. Silvanus was a divinity of the fields and forests. It seems rather hard to be condemned to go through life with a name inviting ridicule. But Fulke's is often a queer sense of humour. Of course Sophie wouldn't see the excessive boskiness of the total effect at all.'

'Probably not, poor kid.'

There was silence for a few moments. Tommy could be observed wheeling a barrow away into the middle distance. Penelope, too, had now sat down on the bench.

'I must tell you something,' Penelope said. 'It's shameful not to have done it long ago. Fulke's wasn't a shot-gun marriage. But there's another common term that conceivably fits. It was on a rebound. From me.'

'It happened at that awful school play,' Penelope said slowly. 'Or just after it was over. Fulke came over from France to see it, you know, on the cock-and-bull strength of having a grandmother who was an Old Girl, or some such nonsense. There we were, with the paint wiped off our faces but still all dressed up, at a party for the parents and people. The senior girls all having glasses of sherry in the presence of their admiring papas and mamas. So there *I* was—pretending, I suppose, to be an Elizabethan boy pretending to be an Elizabethan girl pretending to be an Elizabethan young man. Doublet and hose and a little dagger and a hat with a big feather. Fulke came up to me and said, "Ganymede, will you marry me?" It was a shock. You see, I was rather in love with Fulke. And I didn't for a moment think it was a silly joke. He meant it—quite desperately.'

'And then?'

'I said, "No". Just that—and it was quite desperate too. He believed me at once, and something that came to me as acutely painful happened to his face. But it was only a kind of dark flush. He turned away, and I think he left the party at once. I've never spoken to him, or seen him, since. And he was married to Sophie Dix—I believe with all the trimmings—within two or three months.'

Miss Quillinan took time to digest this, and even to wonder whether another marriage might be described as a kind of rebound in slow motion.

'Penelope,' she then asked, 'did you understand yourself?'

'No, not a bit. It was just some deep thing. And it felt like being suddenly dropped into one of those deep-freezes. I'm not sure I haven't felt a little frozen ever since.'

At this point, and perhaps to the relief of both the young women, there came an interruption to their talk. Penelope's father and his friend Mrs Martin had turned a corner of the vicarage garden and were before them. And as there happened to be a couple of deck-chairs close at hand, the two elders drew them forward and sat down on them in a companionable way. Mrs Martin nowadays spent quite as much time at the vicarage as when Penelope had been her pupil. Penelope had become the house's mistress (if in a slightly unusual fashion), and her former governess now ranked as the household's most intimate friend. That she was also its closest observer was very likely too. The years were dealing with her more kindly than with her former employer—perhaps because she didn't pay too much attention to their passing.

Mr Rich, although he had sat down with every appearance of comfort, almost at once took out his watch and studied it with anxiety.

'Where is Caspar?' he asked. 'I hope he didn't miss mass today?'

'He certainly didn't miss mass. And he's in his study, correcting some proofs.' Penelope had answered patiently, for—as all three knew—here was one of her father's oddities. Once so offended by Caspar's perversion to Rome, he was now regularly apprehensive lest his son-in-law's religious inquiries should lead to some further course of untoward conduct. Too much interest in religion struck Mr Rich as an unwholesome thing, somewhat akin to being excessively concerned about the state of one's inside. His father's generation of clerics had been much troubled by the business of losing their faith; there had been upheavals within families, and bishops burdened by the need unobtrusively to arrange this or that. Fanatical parsons—and not always all that young—had even walked out on their jobs, to live on what a later age would come to call the dole. But on the whole the Anglican church had coped—and could still cope—fairly well— turning on some high-powered professor of theology, for example, to analyse what 'faith' is, after all. Of course the papists were up to that sort of thing too. But Mr Rich had a dim idea that, even with a member of the laity, they regarded such fallings away as much more calamitous. And his son-in-law Caspar, although not exactly a towering figure in the regard of the Vatican, was earning a respectable place among his own lot. If he did a spectacular back-sliding, there might be an extremely disagreeable situation. It wouldn't, indeed, affect Caspar's economic standing, which was virtually non-existent, so far as Mr Rich could see. But he himself, although wholly innocent, might be brought into the picture—as having yanked Caspar out of Rome, so to speak, without successfully restoring him to Canterbury. It was a disturbing thought.

That his daughter might have disturbing thoughts, and have occasioned them equally in her schoolfellow, was not in Mr Rich's mind. Mrs Martin was in different case: aware that between these two young women something had been going on. She hoped—and believed—it wasn't anything to be really alarmed about. Penelope hadn't been confessing to Dora that her marriage had proved distinctly dull. Still less could she have announced it to be a *mariage blanc*, since Mrs Martin knew it to be nothing of the sort. Something had not perhaps ignited quite as it should, but a certain warmth of growing affection was certainly there. Thirty years ahead, if they both lived so long, Penelope and Caspar would be a pair indissolubly wed.

But Mrs Martin was not wholly confident about the salubrity of Dora Quillinan as a possible confidant of her late pupil in this sphere. She liked Dora, and judged her to be without any tendency to rash speech or action. But she was very much a modern girl, and with a consequent frankness that somehow only emphasized a touch of the enigmatic about her own intimate life. And to be modern was to elevate certain aspects of sexuality to a position in which rather damaging topplings-over became a hazard not to be ignored. Mrs Martin felt about sex rather as Mr Rich felt about religion. It ought not to be inordinately brooded on.

That this sort of thing was now revolving in the former governess's head was no doubt the consequence of a perception that some unusual confidence had been going on when she and the vicar had interrupted it. But nothing of the kind, of course, was within the range of the vicar's own observation.

'I've been hoping to find Caspar,' Mr Rich said, 'because something of considerable interest has occurred to me, and I'm sure he would be glad to hear about it. Let me explain.' Mr Rich paused to glance at each of the three women in turn—and perhaps with a faint air of intellectual indulgence or condescension such as that instructive person in *The Pilgrim's Progress* may have exhibited when explaining things to Christian's wife with pictures, because she was a woman and it would be easier for her that way. 'Consider,' Mr Rich said, 'a rectangular blank screen, rather like that of the television machine which you, Penelope, have lately introduced into the vicarage. And consider as appearing on this screen a perpendicular straight line— ideally without dimension as being simply the shortest distance between one point and another. The screen itself we may take to represent the continuum.' This was a new term which the vicar, in pursuit of his metaphysical inquiries, had lately taken to using a good deal. 'The straight line is the Present; it moves across the screen— whether at a uniform pace or not, I cannot yet say; and what it leaves behind is the Past, while what lies ahead of it is the Future. Do you follow?'

The ladies said they followed.

'But now consider this. You all three, I believe, possess a sufficiently constant visualizing faculty actually to have seen with your inner eye the simple phenomenon I have just described. But I should be surprised if each of you had not seen that straight line, endowed with the arbitrary signification I have ascribed to it, as moving from left to right and not from right to left. And I believe this to be almost universal. Artists, for example, when predominantly concerned to suggest the movement of persons or objects through space and consequently through time, organize this on their canvas in the manner I have described: in fact from left to right, and not the other way on. So here is a problem worth considering when the nature of Time is our topic. It is this that I must put to Caspar, who probably hasn't thought of it.'

Mr Rich paused here, clearly gratified by his concluding reflection. But no very lively discussion ensued. Mrs Martin had long since come to think about Time much as she thought about sex: one could have too much of it. Penelope and Dora had other horizons in view—or so, to Mrs Martin, it continued to appear. She experienced a sudden strong dislike of that blank screen. It might be an image of the continuum, but it was an image of a vacuum as well. And as they all four stood up and strolled back to the vicarage, it was in the vicarage, surely, that the vacuum lay. An empty nursery—actually several rooms once known as the nursery wing—undoubtedly had something to do with it.

Part Four

IX

TIME, HOWEVER SIMPLY its effluxion may be represented on a blank screen, is a complex affair of hurryings and lingerings, fullness and emptiness, in any individual's experience. Of this Penelope, grown to womanhood, was well aware. Several years had gone by before she had so much as begun to ask herself whether Caspar Ferneydale's evident devotion was something she could respond to; and she had gone on asking herself the question for several years more. And during all this period, and even although a good deal in the way of confidences had been passing between them, she had never ventured to find out whether Caspar had any knowledge of that strange and untimely proposal on Fulke's part. If he had not, she felt obscurely that her own disclosing of it might somehow tell Caspar more than he'd want to know.

Caspar had been the only person to take any positive satisfaction in Fulke's abrupt transforming himself into a married man. She supposed this to have its source in Caspar's religious convictions. Fornications and adulteries, she knew, were not regarded by his sort of theologian as mortal sins if—severally and as they came along—they were promptly confessed and repented of. Fulke's had been a very bad way of life, all the same—particularly since he was a writer whose talents had come to command admiration among his contemporaries. Penelope suspected that it was not any sort of major artist whose offer of marriage (made in that bizarre theatrical context) she had violently shied away from. And she knew that in this estimate she was supported by what might be called the higher critical opinion. Fulke's ambition was to go to the top. But although popular views might be enthusiastic, and the name of Ferneydale receive brilliant illumination at night in Shaftesbury Avenue, he wasn't destined for the top, and must be conscious of the fact. Fulke like his brother, indeed, was going to be a failure in his own way. Penelope's awareness here even added a shade of guilt to her memory of the manner in which she had turned him down. And this, again, may conceivably have influenced her eventually accepting Caspar's suit. There remained for her a formidable aspect in which she found Caspar unexciting and even slightly dull. But she came to know that fate had made her the person who could bring him domestic happiness and security of an order he sorely required. It was here, in fact, that the big test still lay ahead of her.

The eventual wedding had naturally been quite a grand affair. There was a huge marquee on the vicarage lawn, and the resources of the Hall were thrown in too. Fulke and Sophie found it impossible to turn up, so the bridesmaids were not reinforced by the oddly named Silvan in the character of a seven-year-old page. After the reception Penelope and Caspar drove to Heathrow, took a late plane to Pisa, and were in Assisi on the following day. It happened that Caspar had never visited this celebrated city, and he felt that there was a great deal of ground to cover. Thus St Francis and Giotto had their prominent place in the pleasures of his honeymoon.

James Ferneydale, that harassed City man and model country squire, had been well-pleased with both his sons' matches, but on two distinct accounts. In Sophie Dix Fulke had married the only child of another business man: one unquestionably of very considerable fortune. Like Fulke himself in the earlier stages of his career, Fulke's father held a poor opinion of authorship as a gateway to permanent prosperity, and he therefore regarded the acquisition of a substantial heiress as a measure of commendable prudence in the marital way. With Caspar it was otherwise. If anybody needed a wife with money it was Caspar, and Penelope Rich had no more than a small private income which had come to her from an aunt. But Mr Ferneydale owned a romantic streak. A daughter-in-law whose ancestors had been among the greatest in the land many centuries ago strongly appealed to him. Had it been suggested to him that Caspar upon his marriage should assume the name of Rich-Ferneydale or Ferneydale-Rich he would have seen nothing absurd in the idea.

In fact Mr Ferneydale, who liked to be proud of things, contrived to be proud of his two sons, despite the incomprehensible nature of their predominant interests. He was thus always prepared to talk about them, although on Fulke he was often singularly without up-to-date information. Caspar, dwelling as he did only beyond a hedge and a ha-ha, was better documented from week to week. But then Caspar's weeks seemed to pass in a notably uneventful way.

By this time Dr Hurcomb had retired from practice, and the returned Charles Gaston had become the medical man relied upon both at the Hall and the vicarage. Altough in his mid-thirties, and thus much of an age with Fulke and Caspar, he was still known as 'young Dr Gaston' in the district at large. This was perhaps because his looks were of the sort that wear well, and also perhaps as a consequence of his having remained unmarried. Nobody knew why he had retained this condition, but it was believed by some that had Penelope Rich not become Mrs Caspar Ferneydale during one of Gaston's absences abroad some different fate might have befallen her. However that may have been, had Penelope's marriage not taken her in large measure beyond her father's jurisdiction, the vicar might have looked with disfavour upon Charles Gaston's standing in what might at any time become an intimate professional relationship with his daughter. Mr Rich would naturally envisage a physician of the silver-haired sort as appropriately attending the bedside of any young woman brought up to due standards of modesty. But Caspar, although old-fashioned in many of his attitudes, was without this feeling, and moreover believed that much of Gaston's travelling around was in the interest of remaining conversant with current advances in scientific medicine as many general practitioners (such as old Hurcomb) were not. And with Gaston personally the vicar got on very well. The doctor was a cultivated man, widely-read, and with rather more than Caspar's skill in conversing on intellectual topics with a wary regard for the confined knowledge and intellectual limitations of an elderly and rather lazy country parson. Gaston knew all about the vicar's interest in Time and his naïve belief that he was incubating a significant contribution to our understanding of it. He could even put Mr Rich in the way of reading what other thinkers were finding to say on this perplexing topic.

Dr Gaston got on well, too, with James Ferneydale. If brought in to take a look at an aged parlourmaid who had gone inconveniently wheezy when handing vegetables, or an outdoor man beginning to go wrong at the knees, he would always find leisure for a friendly but properly deferential chat with the master of the household. The deference was, of course, of a formal sort. In fact it had transpired that Charles Gaston, in addition to having attained a higher reputation in his profession than had been supposed, owned an uncle who was a very considerable landowner in a neighbouring county. Mr Rich had been heard to remark that the young man, despite his modest station, was after all a bird of one's own feather.

Gaston possessed, too, other qualifications of the social sort. He was already the senior member of what was coming to be known as a group practice, and as a result was able to treat himself to absences of considerable duration. He liked travel, and could talk entertainingly about various places and peoples. The gift of scientific curiosity seemed with him to spill over into a general interest in the main-springs of human behaviour wherever he encountered them. Here he had perhaps a link with Fulke Ferneydale, whose profession lay in that sort of thing. So the two men had remained on familiar terms, meeting up with one another from time to time in places remote from Mallows. In fact it was from Charles Gaston that the elder Fer-neydales frequently received a first intimation of the current activities of their elder son. It wasn't that Fulke conducted himself as if alienated from his parents. But he did appear to find little occasion to communicate with them on interests and activities remote from their own.

'At last,' Gaston told Mr Ferneydale on returning from one of his continental jaunts, 'I've seen your son's house in the Dordogne. It's a modest affair, but with a magnificent view for that fairly tame part of France. And surprisingly secluded, since its own woodlands appear to extend indefinitely in every direction. I wonder how he found it. Do you happen to know?'

'No I don't. Fulke had been there for some time before we so much as heard of it.' Mr Ferneydale appeared to make this announcement more with satisfaction than otherwise.

'He must at least have sent you photographs of the house and the view from it.' Gaston paused for a moment, as if wondering whether to continue this conversation. He was now glancing with some attention at James Ferneydale. 'Fulke was a keen photographer, wouldn't you say?'

'I know nothing about that, either. Hearing about the existence of the place was the first hint we had that the boy had been doing really well. But I'm surprised to hear that it's secluded and out-of-the-way. That doesn't sound to be Fulke's style.'

'He has certainly been doing really well.'

'Yes, indeed. He was lucky enough to tumble quite early on to an important key to success.'

'What would that have been, Ferneydale?'

'Diversification, Gaston. He hit on that.' James Ferneydale now spoke on his familiar note of paternal pride. 'It's going to be the vital thing, if you ask me, for more than a decade ahead. I insist on it to all my fellow directors in one concern or another. "Diversify," I say. "Go for cement like mad, if you like. But get a grip on the chemical fertilizers, and on all those new leisure-time enterprises as well."'

'I'm sure that's wise. But Fulke's not in cement and nitrates and holiday camps, is he?'

'Of course not. He'd make damn-all of them. With Fulke it's just novels and the theatre. Not specializing, but keeping going at both. They support one another in that type of market. No over-production in one product or the other.'

'That must certainly be so.' Gaston glanced curiously at his host—much as a lepidopterist might glance at a particularly fine specimen of a not particularly uncommon butterfly. 'And as for seclusion and near-solitude, you're perfectly right. But Fulke doesn't appear to spend all that time in this villa. He has to be observing people, since he believes that to be his business. But diversifying there, too. At present he seems to be after high life. The jet set, as they say. And he collects his specimens there much further south. St Tropez, for example. It's going to be the locale of his next play. Sophie and Silvan live in this place in the Dordogne at present, and Fulke comes and goes.'

'What's the child like, Gaston?' James Ferneydale's interest had quickened. He possessed, after all, only one grandchild to date.

'A determined little fellow, I'd say.'

'I'm glad to hear that. It's essential, if one's going to get on. We're in an increasingly competitive world. Damnably ticklish markets everywhere.'

'But they were all three there when I visited the place. Which made it all the odder.'

'Odder?' Mr Ferneydale was perplexed, which was not unnatural. Gaston had given this last remark the character of information involuntary and unpremeditated—and had again looked at Fulke's father sharply at the same time.

'Just the family and a couple of servants.' This came from Gaston as if it was not in the least an inconsequent reply. 'Oh, and a young secretary, whose name I forget.'

Mr Ferneydale frowned. He was clearly wondering whether his son, whom he could scarcely suppose to be by nature strictly monogamous, was undesirably familiar with this nameless female assistant. But he made no further inquiry—with the result that there was a pause in the conversation. When Charles Gaston resumed it, he seemed unconscious of any abrupt change of topic.

'I always think,' he said, 'that Fulke's undoubted success as a writer is the more remarkable in the light of certain limitations he owns in that line. No doubt they have occurred to you.'

'I don't know anything about that.' James Ferneydale was displeased. 'It's not *my* line, you know. So just what are you talking about?'

'Fulke, as we've been agreeing, is endlessly interested in people. There's a sense in which he's a tiptop observer. But he's definitely not an empathic type.'

'What the devil does that mean?'

'Say that he lacks a sixth sense. He doesn't intuitively get into people. So he can sometimes get them wrong. It's no great disability for his sort of writing. But I suppose it's what the highbrow critics have a nose for when they rather turn him down.'

Mr Ferneydale knew nothing about the highbrow critics. But he felt that this young doctor was momentarily one of them. He may have felt, too, that there was an obscurely probing component involved in this whole talk. He was relieved when Charles Gaston took his departure on his morning's round of domiciliary visiting.

Gaston's next call was to be at the vicarage, where Mr Rich was suffering some vexatious minor complaint which he insisted on describing as an attack of the gout. The doctor made his way there on foot, being prompted to the exercise by that mid-thirties persuasion that thought must be given to keeping fit. There was no longer much tennis played at either the Hall or the vicarage—and as for bathing in the glorified duck-pond it simply hadn't happened again since Fulke had contrived that whimsical occasion a dozen years before. Gaston as he walked wondered whether memory and later knowledge were betraying him when he seemed to recall a certain momentary curiosity as having attended that event. And he was further reminded of it now by encountering in the grounds of the vicarage somebody whose acquaintance he had first made round about that time. This was Tommy Elbrow, the vicar's gardener, who was wheeling a leisured barrow around the place much as he had been doing ever since. Or not quite that, since Tommy had for a short period gone as a soldier, not liked it, and managed to get out. He had brought back with him, Gaston reflected, a touch of cynicism other than of the common rustic sort. But he was a patient—or his wife and child were patients—and the doctor paused to have a word with him now.

'Tommy,' he said, 'it's nice to see some unchanging things at Mallows in this alarmingly changing world. Here's you and here's me, both trundling on our rounds as of old. My barrow's a bit the heavier, perhaps. That's all.' Tommy Elbrow, Gaston knew, had a fondness for deeply philosophical reflections of this sort. It might almost be said that, as if infected by his employer's master interest, his own meditations were of Time and what it did to one.

'Changes of sorts there have been here, too,' Tommy said, dropping the handles of his barrow with satisfaction. 'And none for the better, to my mind. Begging your pardon, Doctor.'

'Of just what sort, Tommy? You yourself have got a wife and a fine child now.'

'And not all that more to keep them on. Money's short among my sort. And among the gentry too, it seems. Look at them at the Hall. Paring the cheese, in a quiet way. Squire—as he likes to be called—keeps losing an outdoor man, and no true explanation offered. It's why I'm sent to lend a hand there, every so often. "Lend a hand" is Mr Rich's word for it. But it's hiring me out, an' you ask me.'

'Is that so, now?' No inclination to snub this improper trend in Tommy's talk was evident in Charles Gaston's tone. The pre-army Tommy, he judged, would not so readily have disclosed some smouldering resentment in face of the social order. 'But Mr Ferneydale and the vicar are very old friends. I'd doubt there being any financial motive in your being asked to have a go occasionally at that uncommonly long drive.'

'As you say, Doctor.' Tommy offered this acquiescence with detectably factitious respect, and made to take up his barrow again. But this kind of talk attracted him, and he thought better of it. 'Not that the rich is to be envied,' he said, 'or strung up on lamp-posts as the Commies would have it. They have their own troubles, if you ask me.'

'That's very true. Care isn't to be banished by having what looks good in a bank.'

'Nor boredom neither.' Tommy Elbrow surprisingly broadened the discussion. 'It's a dull life up there at the Hall, just as it is over here at the vicarage. Take Miss Penelope, for instance, as we used to call her. That gay she used to be—but quiet as quiet now. And vicar and Mr Caspar both glooming round over things too deep for them. That I can see, maybe if others don't.'

'I'm sorry to hear it. But quiet lives are often the happiest. The world's hurly-burly can be not all that fun. And you came out of it yourself in a way when you left the forces and returned here.'

'Fair enough.' Tommy put a hand in a pocket and produced a pipe, no doubt a legitimate mid-morning indulgence. 'But take the Hall, too, Doctor. With Mr Ferneydale away on his business a power of the time, and his lady more like a mouse than ever, the Big House be like church on weekdays, with no more nor a sparrow or two trapped and fluttering around it. There was more life to it when the young gentlemen *were* young, and things went on. Even the cricket—but perhaps it was afore your time here—was something.'

'There used to be cricket, did there?'

'Aye—and we all had to turn out for it. And there was always a bit of gossip about goings-on over there. Not that Mr Caspar was ever what you'd call a bright spark. Too religious for it, folk said. Mr Fulke—him that we seldom see glimpse of now—he was different.'

'I suppose he was.' Dr Gaston had a prudent instinct to break off this not quite seemly talk, but failed to obey it. He was interested in what the Mallows world had once thought of the young Fulke Ferneydale. 'It's only natural we don't see much of Mr Fulke now,' he said. 'He's having a great success these days.'

'I don't know as how he was all that successful *then*. Not that there weren't girls about the village who were plain mad about him.'

'Were there, indeed.'

'Yes—but they weren't always the ones he was after. There were some as shied away at once; who wouldn't stand for so much as a quick cuddle with him—like a housemaid in a corridor of the Hall, it might be.'

'It's the privilege of a woman to pick and choose, Tommy.' Gaston made this return to philosophic generality with an encouraging intention. 'Mr Fulke couldn't have been too upset by that.'

'By one thing or another he was often upset, if you ask me. Of the kind that isn't at ease with himself, Mr Fulke is.'

'You're recalling him at an awkward age. He probably has more self-confidence now, and is the easier as a result.' Gaston didn't add that he had himself lately had an opportunity to judge. Such a statement of sustained familiarity with the subject of their discussion might shut Tommy up. And this he didn't want quite yet.

'But he had his resources,' Tommy said suddenly. 'Versatile, Mr Fulke is.'

This term struck Gaston as a surprising one for Mr Rich's gardener to command, and a moment went by before he recalled a sense it carried in current demotic speech. So here was a small investigation abruptly concluded. He offered Tommy no more than a few further casual words, and resumed his walk to the vicarage.

Penelope Ferneydale was in her father's bedroom when Dr Gaston was shown in. She had of late made it part of her business to transcribe or type—and where possible to set in some sort of order—such notes towards his great work as Mr Rich jotted down from time to time. This she had been engaged in now, but she at once gathered her papers together, as if not eager that the vicar should rummage among them for a topic of discourse. She did not, however, then hurry to leave the room, it being clear to her that her father's ailment was in no need of urgent medical attention.

Mr Rich proved, among other vexations, to have been kept awake by a nightingale, although he managed jocularly to admit that disapprobation of such nocturnal entertainment was a reaction wholly unsanctioned in literature.

'Ah!' Dr Gaston said. 'The nightingale you'd like, vicar, is the one in Yeats's poem.'

'Ah!' Mr Rich echoed cautiously. 'Yeats's poem. I'm not sure that for the moment the memory of it doesn't escape me.'

'I take his bird to be an automaton, so you could switch it off and on as you pleased. And it sings to lords and ladies of Byzantium, you'll remember, very much your sort of thing. Of what is past, or passing, or to come.' Achieving this little joke, Gaston had to wonder whether the vicar's daughter liked her father being made fun of even in this gentle way. Certainly Penelope remained entirely grave. But, unlike her father, she knew the poem.

'Set upon a golden bough,' she said. 'It's a little excessive in the Fabergé fashion. And I wonder how many of those Byzantine lords and ladies were to find what was to come anything much to make a song about.'

This was a reflection on the sombre side, but Penelope offered it with composure and a faint smile. She was a woman who was never to be charged, it seemed to Gaston, with any hint of discontent before what even Tommy Elbrow—and from a vantage-point no nearer than his wheelbarrow—could distinguish as a damnably dull life. At least she had managed to develop all the appearance of a mature personality, finding her rewards and fulfilments where she might. The doctor had a poor idea of Caspar Ferneydale as a reward and fulfilment. But, of course, he was prejudiced, and one never really knew. Marriage was very much a mystery. A scribbler like Caspar's brother could write whole plays and novels purporting to reveal its depths and shallows while yet being as much at sea as anybody before one or another specific instance of the conundrum.

' "Of what is past, or passing, or to come",' Mr Rich repeated from his unnecessary sick-bed. 'That is very fine. I must consider corresponding with him.'

'With Yeats? I'm afraid it would be a little late in the day, vicar. He must have died round about the year in which Penelope was born.'

'Dear me! There are matters, I fear, in which I am becoming sadly out of date.' Mr Rich said this not at all as if any sadness actually afflicted him; indeed almost with the complacence of an ageing man resigned to grasping senescence as his bride. But Gaston was annoyed with himself, there having been something clumsy in even an oblique reference to Mrs Caspar Ferneydale's age. Penelope, although still a young woman in any common count, was well advanced within a woman's normal child-bearing span. But Penelope was unoffended. Things had so fallen out, Gaston believed, that the nature of his feeling for the vicar's daughter must remain unexpressed for ever. But perhaps Penelope herself suspected it, and treated him in consequence with a circumspect warmth of regard. There was something of this in her present bearing. She remained easily talking to him for a few minutes before quitting the room so that medical consultation could begin.

It was an unnecessary ritual, but would cost Mr Rich a guinea, all the same. There was nothing wrong with the man—or nothing immediately wrong. But Gaston didn't share his predecessor's view that the vicar was booked for any notable longevity. Several further small cerebral incidents were on the record since the one that had occasioned the child Penelope's first alarm. And listening to the vicar's latest piece of valetudinarian talk now, Gaston found himself speculating on what financial circumstances would attend his patient's sudden death. Had Caspar Ferneydale any money to speak of as his own? Penelope, he had heard it surmised, would be not without a jointure—if that was the correct term—of something more than the pin-money order. But it mightn't be much. There might even come a state of affairs when she was simply her father-in-law's pensioner, and thus necessarily a participant in what Tommy had called the cheese-paring at Mallows Hall.

'Do you know,' Mr Rich suddenly asked—his interest in his own inside lapsing for a moment—'that the faster an aeroplane travels the shorter it becomes from tip to tail? There's considerable theoretical significance in that. I must think about it.'

'If it travelled very fast indeed would it reach a kind of vanishing point, or even a state of non-existence?' Gaston put this question as seriously as if he were addressing Albert Einstein, or some scientist of similar calibre. He was accustomed to receiving from the vicar just this sort of muddled resultance from dabbling in matters astronomically beyond his understanding. 'Turn over on your tummy for a moment, will you? And take a long breath and hold it.'

This got Mr Rich successfully back to the more urgent business on hand, and in a few more minutes the doctor was able to leave him in a reasonably contented condition. But the old man's mind, he judged, was undoubtedly destined to go pop one day. Meanwhile, he couldn't be a housemate of the easiest sort. Gaston found himself indulging a sharp urge to contrive some chivalric means of rescuing Mrs Caspar Ferneydale from this dead-end place. Penelope had, of course, the resource of being active in good works around the parish, as must many clergymen's daughters more or less similarly stranded. But Gaston felt impatient and irritated. It was in this mood that he ran into Penelope's husband.

Caspar was taking a turn in the vicarage garden. He had a drab-coloured journal under his arm. It doubtless contained, Gaston thought, this serious scholar's own sort of nonsense, remote from anything concerning the variable length of aeroplanes.

'I've left my car in the stable-yard at the Hall,' Gaston said. 'Walk over with me. Or rather, since it's such a lovely day, let's make a detour through the park, Caspar.'

'Yes, by all means.' Caspar, if surprised, was also gratified. Here, he might have been feeling, was a busy man inviting his company. It seemed to Gaston that Caspar Ferneydale must be a lonely fellow in his own way. He had made a small name for himself in circles Gaston knew little about, but he must nevertheless strongly feel that his was a disregarded voice. So there was an element of benevolence in Gaston's proposal. But a further feeling was at work. The minds of Riches and Ferneydales alike appeared clouded by a good deal of ignorance. And ignorance was always dangerous, and the struggle against it was what science was about. Gaston believed in achieving clarity—even, as now, within a domestic context with which his own connection was less intimate than he would have wished. But he was aware that there was a certain hazard in this, and that he must beware of behaving like some fatal Ibsenite character convinced that a truth must be brought into the open, come what may.

'I had a chat with your father this morning,' he said when he and Caspar had gained the park. 'I gave him some account of Fulke's villa in the Dordogne. It's rather a pleasant spot, don't you think?'

'I've never been there—any more than my parents have.'

'Well, it is a bit out of the way.' Gaston said this easily, as a man might do who wants to pass lightly over some mildly embarrassing disclosure. This had the effect of a little drawing Caspar out.

'As he has had the place for so many years,' he said, 'it sounds rather like a rift in the family, I suppose. But there's nothing of the kind. It's just a matter of a difference of interests, and of Fulke going his own way. When we were both younger—and particularly when we were undergraduates—he and I were a good deal in one another's confidence. But I confess that to have rather faded out. Do you know, Charles? I believe it's partly because I had ambitions for Fulke which he feels he hasn't justified. Not that they weren't his own ambitions. I wanted his name to be like Hardy's, or somebody of that sort.'

'Well, at least he hasn't turned out a merely popular writer. Fulke is just on the fringe, wouldn't you say? Just short of being received by the mandarins of criticism. Peculiarly galling, come to think of it.' Gaston was now directing the walk he had proposed, and it was in the direction of the centre of the park. 'I never had a brother myself,' he said, 'so I don't know what brothers tell each other. Can you remember'—this came from Gaston as a merely whimsical start of mind—'anything particularly astounding that your brother offered up as a confession to you?'

'I think it was when he told me about having his first woman.' Caspar Ferneydale produced this without a moment's hesitation, since he too was a devotee of truth after his own fashion. 'It was something horribly low and crude, but I suppose more young men have gone through it than not. He had a whore in Paris—but it was mixed up in some way I've forgotten with a glimpse or vision of much less unpolished ungodliness. Anyway, it set him mad about women. I think even my parents know how, in that direction, he was leading a pretty dissolute life. And I had hoped his marriage would put an end to that state of affairs. Or at least put a brake on it. I hope it has.'

'I don't recall Sophie Dix as ever having been likely to remain a charmer for very long. Good Lord! We've come quite a way. Here's your ancestral lake, Caspar. I say—do you remember that bathing party?'

'Very well, Charles. But I don't think I'd care to repeat it now.'

This was an unsurprising remark. Even as a confessed duck-pond the expanse of water before them cut a poor figure. Its surface was scummy; any close approach to it would have been much impeded by hemlock and thistle; and something was happening in its inconsiderable depth which was occasioning a bad smell. The diving board had vanished. The little bathing hut was without a roof.

'I don't think anything of the sort ever happened here again,' Caspar said suddenly and not without agitation. 'Fulke got it up to please Penelope. I don't know whether it did.' Caspar paused on this. 'I have a notion,' he blurted out, 'that he wanted to marry her. When she was a schoolgirl, remember! And there was something about a play. He went to see her in a play at school, although he hadn't the shadow of an excuse for going near the place. He made up some cock-and-bull story about a great-aunt or something. But that somehow finished it. And in no time Fulke had married Sophie.'

'It does sound odd.' After a moment's silent contemplation of the stagnant pool, Gaston risked an impertinent question. 'Has Penelope talked much about all that?'

'I don't think she's ever mentioned it. Perhaps she is unaware of what was happening, and has forgotten all about it.'

'Will Fulke have forgotten all about it? I expect he has, being such a Lothario type.'

'Somehow I think not. I have a queer memory—vague and I can't document it—of Fulke's feeling he had met with some major reverse; with the sort of thing that marks a man.'

Gaston again reacted with a period of silence. He was wondering whether this had gone far enough. But there were things he wanted to know; and there were things he was most curious to know whether Caspar knew. He decided on a frontal attack.

'Caspar,' he said, 'you can't be totally unaware that your brother's sexual make-up isn't quite the common one?'

'What on earth do you mean, Charles?' It took Caspar only a moment to realize that this was a completely dishonest response, and he substituted another. 'How can you know anything about Fulke's sexual constitution?'

'Personal experience, Caspar. That water-party, for a start. It was certainly brought into being for Penelope—or for the Penelope who was to play Rosalind playing Ganymede. Your brother had nothing else in his head. All the same, he spared me a glance. He thought I was asleep, and he spared me a glance. I'd had it elsewhere once or twice before. As a boy.'

'I don't disbelieve you.' Caspar spoke quite quietly now. 'But it can have been no more than a hang-over from our bloody public school. Damn it, Charles! It's notorious that Fulke has been sleeping with women all round the globe.'

'I wouldn't dispute that for a moment. But personal experience takes me a bit further. To my visit to Fulke's villa, Le Colombier, a couple of months ago. He showed me one or two distinctly curious things, and it was again faintly by way of making passes at me. It's rather weird to experience that, actually under a wife's nose, and with a kid playing on the terrace outside. But you see the really amazing fact. It's that Fulke simply doesn't know what's what. Do you understand? He'd got me flat wrong—and that after considerable casual acquaintance. The truth is that Fulke's in a confused bisexual mess. He's what Wilde or somebody wittily called a bimetalist. Actually, there was a scrap of alternative currency already in the house. A young secretary—supposed, incidentally, by your innocent father to be of the female gender. He was called Cyril.'

'I believe there have been several of *them*.' Caspar had opted for candour. 'How about Sophie? Does she know? If so, how can she put up with it?'

'Sophie's so stupid she *mayn't* know. Or perhaps she's thinking of Silvan—who, incidentally, is a tough little brute. It can't be a question of money. We all know that Sophie is quite the heiress in her own right.'

'Charles, you've probably read a lot about this sort of thing. What happens to men such as you say Fulke is when they grow older?'

'They just go on leading tormented lives. And I don't think it can be said to be because of a sense of sin—or not of sin as you yourself probably conceive it. They retain that Don Juan urge to subjugate woman after woman, but there's no deep emotional satisfaction involved. They're in bed with an object: put it that way. But their hope of the both-ways thing, of a satisfying relationship both in bed and out of it—of love, in a word—lies with other men. And they often turn to resenting the universe at large. Unless they're lucky in their bonding and it turns to a permanent thing. It does sometimes happen that way.'

'It's horrible—horrible and tragic.' Caspar Ferneydale was now deeply disturbed. 'My parents must never know. And, although I bear Fulke no ill-will, I can't stand the idea of his ever having given as much as a thought to Penelope.'

'Penelope knows nothing about it?'

'Of course not. How should she? If Fulke actually proposed to her, or something like that, it can't be more than a vague memory of an odd occurrence in near-childhood. Fulke's hardly ever in her head. I can swear to that.'

'You mustn't take too grim a view of it yourself, Caspar.' It seemed to Gaston that he had been foolish in letting his zeal for getting things clear activate an anxiety which had hitherto been no more than slumbering in Caspar's mind. 'These things happen in families quite a lot. I come across them from time to time even in a quiet little practice like mine.'

'Yes, I suppose so.' Caspar had halted, turned round, and appeared to propose returning to the vicarage without further word. But then he changed his mind.

'Charles,' he said urgently, 'you won't talk about these matters with Penelope? It's just not fit that a woman——'

'Quite so.' Gaston cut in rather brusquely with this. 'I can promise not to initiate any discussion of them with your wife.'

'Then that's all right,' Caspar said. But he lingered for a moment before walking away. He had not, perhaps, been wholly satisfied with the form in which this promise had been given to him.

X

THE YEARS LIKE great black oxen tread the world, And God the herdsman goads them on behind. Henry Rich might not have extended his appreciation of Yeats so far as to approve this image, which is scarcely compatible with an orthodox view of the activities of the Deity. But certainly at Mallows the years continued to trudge along, and it is possible that Penelope Ferneydale found them at least dun-coloured for the most part. Mr Rich published a book which had been ingeniously suggested to him by Dr Gaston as a species of occupational therapy: a small anthology of pieces, both in poetry and prose, English, French and Latin, in which the fact that all things flow held a prominent place. *Fugit irreparabile tempus* was the epigraph on the title-page, and Mr Rich gave the whole thing a further touch of learning by referring to it invariably as a *parergon*—a word which sufficiently curious persons looked up in their dictionaries and discovered to mean something like a by-product of graver labours. This rather dreary book was civilly noticed by a number of reviewers.

Caspar also produced his book, and it was received very well indeed in the circles for which it was designed. In fact Caspar looked like coming into his own at last, and it was therefore the sadder that he was killed in a railway accident within a few months of his work being published. Fulke came to the funeral, stayed for a decent number of days with his parents at the Hall, and returned to a life which nobody any longer knew much about. Fulke's writing was declared by the critics to have deteriorated a little, and his fortune was known to have increased a great deal. It was asserted by some—but less on actual evidence than as an inherently probable conjecture—that he was now separated from his wife. Anything more scandalous than this found no circulation at Mallows.

That Penelope had been left childless as well as a widow was a state of affairs striking her father in two lights. It added to the calamity that his daughter should be without even one infant for whom to care. He grieved over this. Yet it was not an altogether unfortunate circumstance, if looked at from a dispassionate and realistic point of view. Penelope might have been left with three pairs of twins. And what came to her through the arrangements made at the time of her marriage, although not paltry, fell short of what might have been desired. It had to be Mr Rich's hope that his daughter, perhaps in two or three years' time, would make a second marriage more satisfactory than the first in point of material interest. There would still be plenty of time for her to bear children in reasonable number.

But this prudent and hopeful thinking did nothing to alter the present fact, which was that Penelope turned thirty was just where, a dozen years before, it had been predicted by some that she was only too likely to end up. She was the childless daughter of a widower of many years' standing, and as that widower was the incumbent of a rural parish, she had more than half the chores of that parish on her hands. Mrs Ferneydale at the Hall helped, but with benevolence rather than activity. She commanded, that is to say, reasonable sums of money, which she applied to charitable uses under Penelope's direction. But these were years in which rural life was changing in various ways; social relations were changing under the impact of social legislation; Penelope found it easy to feel something outmoded and even archaic in the rôle she was called upon to fill.

And during these years nothing much seemed to happen. People were growing older, no doubt, but only in Mr Rich's case could this be called very evident. Charles Gaston, who had so injudiciously brought to the surface of Caspar's mind circumstances which had only vaguely been troubling it, found himself distinctly unsettled by Caspar's death, and in fact revived thoughts about Caspar's widow which would have been entirely idle had Caspar lived. Then—too soon, perhaps, and from his own sense that the years were slipping treacherously by—he asked her to marry him. Penelope's reply was instant and seemingly convinced. It was not her intention, she said, ever to marry again. If she thus saw herself as an inconsolable widow in the Victorian taste it was possibly because she had before her the example of her father, with whom widowerhood seemed now to be a settled thing. Slowly after this, however, her secret feeling came to approximate to that of a princess (or a vicar's daughter) entranced in a tower, obscurely expectant of what didn't turn up. It was a kind of existence in which, paradoxically, those years seemed less to linger than to slip unobtrusively by. On Sundays she frequently found herself joining in a hymn asserting that the daily round, the common task, should furnish all she ought to ask. Several remote relations, hitherto not much bothering about the Mallows Riches, became aware they had a duty to her, and once or twice in a twelvemonth she would pay a family visit, or join in a continental holiday with people she only slightly knew.

Mrs Martin, who had long ago evinced a disposition to look purposively ahead in Penelope's interest, was the one person to seek some radical change in the situation, and to keep in mind the fact that her former pupil was still a young woman, with a life to live which might somehow be advantageously changed from the life she seemed settled in now. The crux of the problem appeared to Mrs Martin's mind to be the vicar. Time, once more, and a certain advancement in her material circumstances following upon deaths and bequests in her family, had turned her into a person of property, and therefore of greater consequence in Mallows and the small world around it. Were she minded, she could even act with some degree of eccentricity without attracting censure. Eventually she decided that nothing but good—meaning Penelope's good—would result were she to supplant the enchanted princess as the mistress of the vicarage and presiding lady in the parish. Elderly people, long known as intimate friends, frequently enter upon mutually supportive and convenient marriages. There was no reason why she should not become, even at this late hour, the second Mrs Henry Rich.

Or there was no reason except Henry Rich himself, a man now older than his years and settled in his ways. But Mrs Martin felt this to be no insuperable obstacle. The main difficulty lay in divining Penelope's inner mind were such a radical change to be revealed as on the domestic carpet. In fact it had to be discussed with Penelope before any action could be taken. Mrs Martin, whose thoughts were never of a facile order, was far from underestimating the difficulty and hazard of this. In the end she discussed it first with Dora Quillinan.

Dora had by this time made the career she had promised herself, and in a business world still unhabituated to seeing a woman's name in a list of company directors. She probably knew more about James

Ferneydale than anybody else did, but she seldom made him a topic of conversation during her visits to the vicarage—which she was still not too preoccupied to pay every now and then. When consulted by Mrs Martin she agreed that something should be done, and that the doing of it could fall well within her own range of activity. She could, as she expressed it, 'float' Penelope into agreeable and reasonably remunerative employment in no time at all.

'But that isn't quite my idea,' Mrs Martin said. 'Penelope still isn't too well off in her own right, but she has quite enough to make do without seeking employment. What I'd like to free her for is a successful second marriage. I had hopes, you know, of Charles Gaston. But that seems to have hung fire.'

'Then Penelope needs a wider field of choice. A job would put her in the way of meeting eligible men in a way that just doesn't happen at Mallows. Ideally, Mrs Martin, her getting a job, and meeting up with the right suitor, and learning that you and her father were proposing to get married, should tumble more or less on top of one another in that order.'

'I see the force of that, Dora.' Mrs Martin also felt uneasy about it, and quickly discovered why. 'I've been forming a plan,' she said. 'And I've drawn you into that plan—which turns it into a conspiracy. I doubt whether one should make plans for other people at all, however much their welfare means to us. Plans should be about things like houses and dividends and literary projects and planting roses. You understand me?'

'I certainly understand you. Making plans for people is a kind of reification, I suppose. Treating them as pawns, or at best as kings and bishops. But it's not an argument that impresses me. I'm more conscious of the fact that any plan takes a measure of time to work out, and that then some unsuspected factor barges in and changes the whole scene. That's always happening in business.'

It happened in the present private affair. Some further months went by, and at the end of them Mr Rich himself proved, rather unexpectedly, to have been addressing his mind to the same problem as was confronting the ladies. The vicar was conceivably a self-indulgent man to a degree a little beyond the average. But he was also a conscientious parent: a character in which he has already been exhibited in those early anxieties in the field of female education. It was his slow discovery that he was sacrificing his daughter to his own domestic ease. The germ of this perception had come to him when Charles Gaston had inadvertently half-revealed to him the fact of his having made Penelope that offer of marriage. Mr Rich found himself disappointed rather than relieved when nothing further seemed to have come of this, and it appeared to him that he himself must be a factor in Penelope's hanging back. He had to conclude that his dependence on his daughter, domestically and as a helpmeet in his parochial labours, must be where the impediment lay, and he saw that to rectify this state of affairs there was a clear instrument close to his hand: in the room with him, in fact, as often as Mrs Martin visited the vicarage. After long deliberation, therefore, he took the plunge. He held a serious conversation with the chosen lady, and at its close found that he had specifically proposed that rational and (it was to be hoped) mutually agreeable arrangement over which Mrs Martin had been hesitating, as she knew, too long. The marriage was to take place, and Penelope thereby to be released into some vaguely conceived larger world—this perhaps under the superintendence of the useful and reliable Dora Quillinan.

As with many rational schemes designed to operate within the obscure field of the human heart, the result didn't quite answer to expectation. Perhaps this was in part because the actual sequence of events was not as Dora had envisaged it. More significantly, Penelope saw what was going on, and took no particular pleasure in the idea that rescue work was in hand. She had been doing everything that her situation required uncomplainingly and efficiently, and she was humiliated by the thought that she had perhaps been betraying any sense of frustration or hankering after a different manner of life. Moreover the notion of a job (which she divined as intended to bring her into promising contact with eligible suitors) was slow to mature. Some sort of preliminary secretarial training there would have to be, which would be almost like going back to school. So all that happened for some time was that Penelope lived on as the second, rather than the first, lady of the vicarage. The situation was reasonably harmonious, but it could be that without being entirely comfortable, all the same.

And then there occurred the first event in Penelope's life justly to be described as strange to the point of amazement. Fulke Ferneydale died abroad after what appeared to have been a fairly long illness. His will, when its contents were revealed, held nothing unusual in any major regard. To his wife, Sophie Ferneydale, whether because of some estrangement or not, he left little: a disposition of things not particularly out of the way, since Sophie was a rich woman in her own right. The bulk of his fortune was held in trust for his son, Silvan. There were various minor bequests. But one bequest couldn't quite be described as that. To his sister-in-law, Penelope Ferneydale, he left a small income for life. And he left her, too, as her absolute property, his villa in France.

XI

'BUT THERE'S NOTHING uncommon about it at all,' Mrs Henry Rich said. She spoke with just that hint of patience which she had allowed herself when her pupil was being unreasonable long ago. That hadn't been often. Reasonableness was one of Penelope's endowments. Yet she wasn't being altogether reasonable now. Her first reaction to the news of her unexpected inheritance was simply that she had been singled out for undeserved and undesired notoriety.

'At least it's ludicrous,' she now said. 'It makes me remember that Fulke went in for ridiculous jokes.'

'Penelope, dear, that's absurd. Listen to the facts. It's hard nowadays for even a very successful writer or artist to build up a fortune—even with big cheques dropping in on him month after month. But Fulke was enough his father's son to know just how. Living now in this country and now in that, and having advisers who knew all about what they call tax havens. I don't say it's edifying, but it's the way of that sort of world. And you see, although they were so different in temperament, he and Caspar were fond of one another. And Caspar had made no money at all out of thinking and writing of a much more serious sort than Fulke's. Fulke knew that; knew that his success hadn't been at the level he had promised himself when young. Fulke wasn't insensitive to considerations of that sort. It would be unjust to him to suppose so. Don't you agree, Penelope?'

'I suppose I'm prepared to—provisionally.'

'Very well. Because of his affection for his brother——'

'Stop, Mary—please stop.' This was now Penelope's manner of address to her former governess and present stepmother. 'There's something you don't know. I think only Dora knows it. Fulke Ferneydale once proposed marriage to me.'

'After proposing to be divorced by Sophie? I can't believe it.'

'You don't have to. It was before Sophie, and when I was still at school. Caspar may have had an inkling of it, although I never mentioned it to him.'

'Was *that* some kind of joke?' Mrs Rich was momentarily put to a stand by this extraordinary information.

'It was odd, but it wasn't a joke. He was quite serious. And I think I'd been inclined to admire Fulke in a childish way. But I knew at once I wasn't going to marry him, either there and then or later on. So I said so, and that ended it, and in time it pretty well went out of my head. You see, we never ran into one another again, and all I retained was a feeling that I had upset or mortified him surprisingly. So you see how disconcerting it makes what has happened now.'

'I see nothing of the kind. Fulke, with all that wealth, would naturally have left something to his brother. And Caspar being dead, he would equally naturally do something for his widow, particularly if it was plain she wasn't going to be too well off. And if long ago, and as a very young man, he'd had this strain of romantic feeling for you as a schoolgirl, that simply adds to the naturalness of his eventual bequest. I don't think, Penelope, that there is anything you need feel strange about it.'

'But a house in France! It's not as if I'd ever seen the place, or owned any associations with it.'

'That makes it a little curious, I agree. It suggests Fulke as rather prompted to direct your life. It's as if he were saying, "Here's something new, Penelope. Have a go at it."'

'But he has been a stranger for years and years, on no sort of terms entitling him to say anything of the sort.'

'He was your brother-in-law. So you must go and take a look at the place, even if you decide to part with it at once. It would be almost feeble to do anything less than that.'

'Oh, yes—I'll go.' Penelope hadn't liked this. 'At once, in fact—and perhaps see French lawyers and people.' Penelope paused, but only for a moment, for she knew what Mrs Rich was about to suggest. 'And alone,' she said. 'The best way to see it through will be that.'

To this resolution of a solitary exploration of Le Colombier Penelope stuck, even when—not unexpectedly—Dora Quillinan offered to accompany her.

'Of course you know your way about France,' Dora said. 'But

144

circumstances have taken me a bit further, and I know my way about the French. That's a different thing from being well up in châteaux and cathedrals, and even knowing when to go for the *prix fixe* meal. I might save you from any number of man-traps.'

'There certainly won't be any of *them*—in one sense of the term, that is.'

'Well, no. I don't see you falling for a French adventurer, abounding in powers of swift and subtle seduction. But in that general direction lie my doubts about the whole thing. The house turns out to be enchanting; you fall in love with it and dig in; and not within a hundred miles of it is there going to be anybody apt and fit to fall in love with *you*. You'll become an expatriate old English widow, occasionally visited by elderly friends from England. It's not what I want for you, because I know it's not what you are and need. There! I've said my say.'

'As you're entitled to, being my oldest friend. I've promised Mary to go and take a look, which is only reasonable. And I want it to be without the hint of a nudge while I'm doing the looking. It's a strange and rather daunting thing to have happened. I even feel, Dora, that there's a mystery about it which I haven't begun to fathom—and that I may do that best on my own. Do you see any sense in that?'

'I do see something obscure in the whole thing. But the world is full of obscurities. You must stick to the practical issues, and I agree that you're capable of doing that on your own. You've been left money, and you've been left a house. But what about all the stuff in it? Is that to be yours too?'

'Yes—and it's a part of the thing that I particularly don't like. Mary points out that the house—which is said to be fairly modest—and the small income with it form something that might properly have gone to Caspar, and may properly go to Caspar's widow. Sophie, who is wealthy, would be unlikely to take exception to it. But Fulke, it seems, was very much the connoisseur from the moment he had the money to set up as one. So Le Colombier may contain heaven knows what.'

'In other words, real trouble. Sophie saying the Cézanne was really hers, and not Fulke's to give away. And sweet little Silvan——'

'Sweet little Silvan must be getting on for grown-up.'

'And Silvan is prepared to swear that yes, it had always been known to be that. Not nice at all, I agree. But you could just gracefully cede anything in dispute. And we know that Fulke owned several places grander than Le Colombier, and that Sophie is in the enjoyment of one of them now. Le Colombier was a working retreat, so far as I can make out. Fulke would keep his showing-off things in his show places.'

'I'd expect that a writer or artist would have his most beautiful and cherished things beside him where he worked. And not, say, on board some glossy yacht in which he went cruising in off times with a gaggle of bounders and high-class tarts.'

'Well, yes.' Dora Quillinan glanced at her friend with some curiosity. 'You resent—don't you?—Fulke's stupidly dissipated life. It's a kind of loyalty, that. Yet you last had words with him when you were seventeen. How odd we are! Human beings in general, I mean.'

'He was the first person I ever knew whom the world knew about too. But only when I was a half-baked adolescent. After that I did really and truly clear him out of my head, even despite that old irresponsible proposal of his. So I agree that fussing over this bequest is a little on the unreasonable side.'

'Well, Penelope, off you go. And I'd drive myself there, if I were you. It doesn't seem a region of France particularly easy to fly to, and you have a perfectly good car eating its head off there in the garage. France is nice for driving in. There's a sense of space and freedom about it, particularly if you keep to the quiet Departmental roads. You'll arrive already feeling in control of the situation. And one other piece of advice, my dear. If you positively take against Le Colombier, don't go straight to the nearest estate agent and flog it there and then. Any piece of house property—and especially in what is becoming something of a rich man's holiday area—is under present conditions a far more permanent asset than a big lump of francs cash down.'

So Penelope packed a suitcase and drove to Southampton a couple of days later. The channel-ferry failed to afford a promising start. She was old enough to remember the small groups of polite children on such vessels in process of undergoing exchange with appropriately selected families abroad. These had now been superseded by hordes of gang-like teen-agers, ceaselessly hallooing as they charged and jostled from stem to stern. They represented, it appeared, a sizeable proportion of the juvenile population of some English town 'twinned' with a French one to which they were proceeding *en masse* for cultural purposes. There were also juke-boxes and fruit-machines, as well as a place where you could play a primitive form of roulette. She had to queue to buy a ticket entitling her to queue for a meal.

Nothing of all this did Penelope take to or find fun. She had escaped growing up as a prig, let alone as a snob, but her instincts and habits were yet on the fastidious side. She had, she told herself, the vicarage on her back, and always would have. She was quite as old as her years and probably a good deal older—certainly too old to be facing with any sense of positive pleasure the total unknown of a house in the Dordogne called Le Colombier. Yet the name, at least, was reassuring. There was a dovecot at Mallows Hall, and she had always found it a most peaceful spot.

The two long days' driving were reassuring too, much as Dora had foretold. There were many things she knew nothing about, and one of them was the kind of regard in which a solitary female motorist would be held. This particular dubiety—doubtless an inheritance, again, from her father's archaic way of conceiving such matters—didn't survive her first stopping for petrol, and had become absurd by the time she foraged for, and consumed by the roadside, her first picnic lunch. She hadn't forgotten a corkscrew, and opening her first half-bottle of wine was an exhilarating experience. She spent the night at Amboise, and wandered around it till it grew dark, full of naïve wonderments. How strange that some people should have lived in that towering château while others cowered in troglodyte dwellings excavated in steeply sloping hills or near-cliffs, and still advertised their doing so with brightly painted front-doors and flower patches outside. How odd that a municipality lining the majestic Loire should conceive that an additional charm to their scene was achieved by vapid music piped to every street corner. How odder still that Leonardo da Vinci should have taken it into his head to die here. Strangest of all was the gargantuan fountain presented by Max Ernst to Michel Debré, and by Debré (expeditiously, one supposed) to this unoffending town—the inhabitants of which, not being given to the *mouvement surréaliste*, had promptly vandalized it in the most atrocious manner.

Sated with these curiosities, Penelope dined on carrot and potato soup, *truite au Vouvray*, and another half-bottle of wine. Then on the next morning the great straight roads received her, with just occasionally those tricky twists and turns through little towns bewilderingly provided with sign-posts to everywhere except the next town to which one wants to go. But these were difficulties not hard to overcome once she had found that very decent French still lurked at the back of her mind. Eventually she arrived at one small town where business had to be transacted. She found an office of indefinite character—a lawyer's, she supposed—in which she was received with considerable respect. Keys were handed to her by the principal functionary in the place, but with what she felt as an obscure intimation that this was a formality only, and that she would have no immediate need to sort out which was which. With marked ceremony, too, she was escorted back to her car, so that she drove off with the sense that Fulke Ferneydale had been judged a man of mark in this district at large.

The road became narrower and winding, skirting wooded slopes through which she had glimpses of water not far below. Then what she knew to be the Vézère and the Dordogne joined their streams almost under her wheels; the road rose steeply above the augmented flood; she knew that Le Colombier now lay only a few kilometres ahead. This was Penelope's first moment of panic, and she had to tell herself sternly that nothing irrevocable was happening to her. She had been more to Fulke Ferneydale than she realized, and he had made her a handsome present as a posthumous token of the fact. His way of life had been totally remote from hers; it had become one in which a great deal of wealth floated around, and in which people floated with it, and would find nothing remarkable in inheriting under some friend's will a little house in the middle of France. To feel panic was absurd. A lively curiosity was what ought to be commanding her.

Penelope had just told herself this when she found that any curiosity she did command was about to be gratified. Straight before her, at a corner of the road, the words 'Le Colombier' were repeated on white wooden posts on either side of a white wooden gate. The gate stood open. Penelope braked, swung her wheel, and in an instant had exchanged ground which was the property of nobody in particular for ground which was the property of herself alone. In a suitcase in the boot of her car were documents that she knew attested the fact in the most incontrovertible manner. The sudden sense of possession which came upon her as she made a cautious and rather bumpy progress up a short drive in indifferent repair took her by surprise. With the exceptions of a room of her own, and books of her own, and unspectacular sums of money trickling into a bank, the notion of proprietorship of any sort had been alien to her. Now there was this. For she had turned a final bend, and Le Colombier was before her.

What she was first aware of was the structure from which the house took its name. The dovecot was evidently of great antiquity, beautiful in itself, and so massive as an assertion of manorial privilege that it must have been the appurtenance of a château, long since vanished, in which dwelt whole armies of retainers passionately addicted to the consumption of pigeon pie. Since then, but unobtrusively, the high conical building appeared to have been transformed into living quarters of a modest sort, since here and there glazed windows had replaced the tunnel-like apertures appropriate to its original denizens. Penelope wondered whether Fulke had turned it into an ultimate sanctum for his literary labours. Then she drove on to look at the house itself. She saw that it was quite modern, although designed after the traditional domestic architecture of the region. She saw, too, that there was nothing showy about it; that it had been contrived, in fact, to look a good deal less spacious than it probably was. The north front, at which she was looking now, would have been a blank brick wall had it not been pierced in the centre by a handsome doorway, beside which hung a bell-rope accompanied by a board carrying the brusque instruction, *Sonnez ici*. Above broad eaves there could just be discerned, as if peering cautiously down at visitors, a line of dormer windows. Le Colombier's unassumingness evidently extended to the possession of no more than an attic type of second storey.

Penelope, who had got out of her car, presumed it would be pointless to ring the bell, no caretaking person having been mentioned to her. So she walked round an angle of the house, and discovered that it was without a regular garden of any sort. What surrounded it was a generous *parterre* of ancient stone; beyond this, and broken only by the drive, was a wide circle of well-tended lawn; and beyond this a yet wider cincture of unmown but not untended grass: this last displaying such an abundance of wild flowers as triumphantly to assert that Nature can be her own gardener with only the hint of a helping hand. Further off lay woodland on every side. But from a broad terrace shaded with abundant vines which ran the entire length of the south front of the house a vista had been created through the nearer trees, while those in the middle distance dipped, as in a deep natural saucer beyond which, far below, was a glimpse of the Dordogne itself: of the Dordogne and a vast champain of cultivated land finally lost amid the blueness of a range of far-off hills.

So this was Le Colombier, her strange inheritance.

XII

But the house itself was yet to be explored, and Penelope turned back to it now. The ground floor presented a long row of identical french windows, and at first all of them appeared to be shuttered. This might well be a normal practice on a hot summer afternoon, but on the present occasion was presumably due to the fact that the dwelling was unoccupied. She felt in her handbag for the bunch of keys she had been given, but as she did so became aware that one of the shutters and the french window behind it were only half-closed. So there, at its eastern end, one could walk straight into the house. For a moment Penelope was alarmed. Nothing had been made clearer to her than the substantial isolation of Le Colombier. It stood, indeed, only a couple of hundred yards from the quiet country road on which its unassuming entrance gate lay, but on every other hand stretched empty woodland which was now hers alone. The nearest dwelling must be half a mile away.

And now she recalled that conversation with Dora Quillinan, only half-serious, about Le Colombier's being conceivably a small treasure-house of collector's pieces of this and that. The villa was a sitting target for burglary—and perhaps there were burglars in it now. But she was already advancing upon the single window when she recalled that slight suggestion she had been given that the keys were not of essential present utility after all. So perhaps there was some sort of *femme de charge* in residence, or at least somebody sent in for the day to make reasonable provision for her arrival. Taking courage from these speculations, she walked straight up to the open window, and entered the house.

She was in a large room, furnished, as she sensed at once, with considerable elegance, but oddly and confusingly lit by the single bar of strong sunlight behind her. Yet this was enough to show her that the room was not untenanted. Near its centre a young man was standing before an easel, and he swung round and confronted her now.

'Oh, hello,' the young man said in English. 'I've just been monkeying around with edges in an odd light. Op art, I suppose they'd call it. Purely academic, and not my sort of thing at all.' He paused for a moment, as if realizing that this, if informative, was scarcely adequate to the situation. 'I say,' he went on, 'you're not Penelope, are you? But of course you are! I knew you were coming, but didn't know it would be so soon. Let's have more light on the state of the case.' This remark was intended in a literal sense, since the young man rapidly pushed back two pairs of shutters and filled the room with sunshine.

'Yes,' Penelope said, 'I am certainly Mrs Ferneydale.'

'That's splendid. Welcome to Le Colombier. I think you'll find all quiet, and everything ship-shape. Although it was only a couple of days ago that I had to repel boarders.'

'Boarders?' Penelope managed no more than this stupid echo because considerably taken up by the appearance and the implications of this strange young man. He was much younger than herself, and very good-looking. Penelope believed herself to be rather prejudiced against good-looking men, and particularly against that odd sub-species among these to whom 'beautiful' was an applicable term. This youth was certainly beautiful, and was certainly going to remain handsome. She was also inclined to dislike male persons in whom a marked ease of manner and conversation too rapidly made itself apparent. So she ought not to have been attracted by this unexpected and so-far anonymous intruder upon her property. The situation, however, wasn't working like that. It was all rather surprising. But she found herself much disposed to accord it the provisional benefit of a doubt.

'Just that. Pirates, you might say. Tiresome Sophie, with her Silvan in tow. A hulking great brute, isn't he?'

'I've never met Silvan Ferneydale.'

'Then you haven't missed much. They simply rang the bell—*Sonnez ici*, you know—and demanded the picture.'

'Not the Cézanne?' Penelope was recalling again that recent conversation with Dora.

'The Modigliani. Silvan declared it to be the property of his Mum, and actually made to take it from the wall. That just couldn't be put

152

up with, and I had to deal with him a shade roughly. No, Penelope, I'm not romancing—slender of frame though you see me to be. Just a spot of karate, followed by something that tends rapidly to hurt quite a lot. Finally I let him bolt howling, with Mum behind him. They haven't a shadow of a legal claim, you know, so we shan't have any nonsense from them again. And now sit down. I'm going to make you some tea.'

Penelope sat down. She had received an instruction, and had obeyed it. This in itself required thinking about. Who was this young man, and what was his function? He was at least to some extent conversant with Ferneydale family affairs, and it had been without any effect of impertinence or presumption that he had addressed her by her christian name. Was he perhaps a Ferneydale of sorts himself—a kind of cousin of her own, for instance, born on the wrong side of one of Fulke's innumerable blankets? Or was his connection with Fulke merely of a professional kind, which had nevertheless taken on a friendly and intimate character? Her thought had gone a little beyond this, and she was on the brink of remembering some name she had once heard mentioned, when the young man reappeared, carrying a tray.

'*Thé parfumé à l'essence de la bergamote,*' he said cheerfully. '*Exporté par Jacksons of Piccadilly.* But *en mousseline,* I'm afraid. Which means tea-bags.'

'Thank you very much.' Having accepted her cup, Penelope decided that the moment for firmness had come. 'May I ask,' she said, 'what is your position here?'

'I suppose it does need a little explaining.' For a moment the young man showed some sign of turning serious. But then his gaiety returned. 'I'd be inclined to put it,' he said, 'that my position is like the Modigliani's or the Cézanne's. I go with the house.'

Penelope found this a disconcerting remark. It had been uttered whimsically or lightly, and perhaps she should have replied, 'Like a washing-machine, you mean, or a billiard-table?' But something made her reject this. 'And does anybody else go with the house?' she asked.

'There's an old woman who comes as well as goes, and who does the washing up. And a boy called André, who looks after the grass. But essentially just me, Penelope. Fulke never had more than one secretary. At a time, that is.'

'Then are you Cyril?' This was the name some casual mention of which had come back to her.

'Cyril? Good heavens, no! I'm Bernie. I never set eyes on Cyril, or so much as knew his surname. Two or three before me, Cyril must have been.'

'I see. My brother-in-law can't have been too fortunate in his secretarial assistance. May I know your surname, please?'

'Huffer. But I'll consider myself snubbed if you call me that way. I'll call you Mrs Ferneydale, and it won't sound friendly at all. Not if we're going to work together. "Bernie" it would have to become, and "Bernie" it had better be now.'

Bernie said this while pouring Penelope more tea. She had held out her cup when it became apparent he proposed to do so. Part of what Bernie had said was perfectly true. He was a good deal her junior, so it would be absurd to address him as if he were an elderly gardener. There was something singular about the whole thing, all the same.

'Very well, then—Bernie. But I don't understand what you said about our working together. Judging from *that*'—and Penelope pointed at the canvas on its easel—'what you are is a professional painter. I don't think amateurs go after quite what you're trying to do there.'

'Well, perhaps not. But one can test oneself, you see, by seeing whether one has the technique to master other people's tricks. Those lines and areas I've been daubing on are perfectly static and inert on the canvas. But I want to make you believe that you see them moving as you look at them. It's fascinating in a way, but even if it succeeds it's no more than a superior form of conjuring. Much like a lot of Fulke's writing, as a matter of fact. He wants to kid us that things created by him are moving when they are not. And at a certain level he gets away with it.'

'I suppose I follow that.' Bernie, it seemed to Penelope, was possessed of rather more of critical intelligence than of simple loyalty to his former employer. 'But you still haven't told me how and why we're to work together.'

'On Fulke's papers. There's a letter about them waiting for you upstairs which I imagine to be similar to one he left for me. He wants

154

the papers to remain in this house—your house—and the copyright in them is vested with you entirely. He hopes we'll sift through them, and prepare a certain amount of them for publication.'

'But it's absurd, Bernie. I read English at Oxford long ago, but I'm not any sort of literary person. It can be nothing but a sick man's fancy.'

'Fulke says—a shade enigmatically for me—that he once tried to place something rather important in your hands, and failed. He wants to do the same with something less important now.'

This small thunderbolt silenced Penelope through her second cup of tea. But when she did speak, it was to the point.

'Bernie, do you yourself much want to take part in this job you talk about? You sound to me as if not all that impressed by Fulke's talent and his success with it. And your association with him seems to have been fairly brief. Do you really want to get to work on his stray papers?'

'I like Le Colombier. And now I like you.'

'That's a frivolous thing to say. You haven't known me for half an hour.'

'Well, in a way I haven't. But my feeling is that here at last you are, and that it would be nice to do the work together. If that sounds silly, I'm sorry. By the way, when I said "Le Colombier" I meant it literally in one sense. I have quarters in the dovecot. And I'll promise, if you like, never to emerge from them before blowing a whistle to let you know. The propriety of the situation shall be unflawed.'

'Whistle or no whistle, it will certainly be that.'

'Sorry again, Penelope. When I'm nervous I tend to produce silly quips. And I'm as nervous as hell. It has all been a bit sudden, for one thing. I suppose you knew—as I didn't—that Fulke rather went in for making quirky wills. Every now and then a new one, with fresh ideas turning up. Quite a gold-mine to his lawyers, Fulke must have been.'

'No, I didn't know—although I was told the effective will was of very recent date.'

'And those letters to be posthumously delivered: it seems that was a thing of his too. The creative impulse getting a bit out of hand, I suppose. But let's drop Fulke for a moment. Do you know what I'm going to do? Leave you for a couple of hours to settle in, and then come over and cook a meal and find a bottle of wine. I've been a pretty good cook for rather a long time. But with wine it was a matter of a crash course with our late friend.'

'Was Fulke——'

'No, Penelope—not another word about Fulke now. There's a lot I want you to know about him—or I think there is—but I must arrange my thoughts on the subject or I'll just muddle him. Would you judge champagne a vulgar and unpromising start to our association?'

'I'm not sure there's going to be an association, Bernie. But I've no doubt whatever that Fulke owes us a bottle of champagne.'

'Good girl! Do you mind my calling you that? I'm beginning to work it out that you must be—but amazingly—a few years older than me. But then I'm very young indeed.'

'Go away, Bernie. That couple of hours not filled with incomprehensible nonsense may remove some of the lines from my brow. But I look forward to my dinner.'

'And there's the same promise of propriety—although I never gave a harder——'

'*Go away!*' Penelope found herself—distinctly with surprise—uttering this command with amusement rather than indignation. Bernie Huffer obeyed it at once. So Penelope was left to make what she could of as strange an encounter as she could remember. She tried to tell herself that 'perky', or even the more demotic 'fresh', was the correct and sufficient epithet for Fulke's late secretary. But she saw that nothing of the sort would quite do. She *had* been amused by Bernie Huffer. And it was undeniably rather a long time since she had been much amused by anybody else.

Bernie proved to be indeed a very good cook, and he produced a dinner much superior to the one Penelope had judged it prudent to order for herself in Amboise. Moreover he was tactful over the champagne, ensuring that the bottle should be empty before she had finished her second glass. His guest (or employer) was left not without misgivings, all the same. Although now a widow who would not again see thirty, she still—as has been remarked—carried around with her at least a residue of her father's persuasions in several fields. Mr Rich would distrust a young man who, being born or at least bred in no sort of menial condition, had turned himself into a competent chef. And Mr Rich would judge it decidedly strange that his daughter should sit down to any sort of meal at all in a secluded situation and the sole company of her late brother-in-law's male secretary. But although such notions did lurk in some corner of Penelope's own mind they didn't greatly trouble her. And she found that Bernie was much more capable of a discreet comportment than her first rather bewildering encounter with him might have suggested.

He provided an amusing preview of the character both of Mme Saval, who came in to clear up and clean around, and of André, who looked after the lawns and the terrace and everything else outside. After this he talked a good deal about Fulke—and on the unstated but perfectly just premise that Penelope's information on this family benefactor was of a sketchy sort. Penelope did know that Fulke's life had been not such as Mallows could approve. It had to be admitted, Bernie said, that Fulke was a man too frequently liable to be fondly overcome with female charm. But he had been a good-hearted chap, and amusing in a variety of ways. At this point, although always waiting to be prompted by some question or other token of interest, Bernie's conversation took on an anecdotal turn. His stories about his late employer were sometimes very funny, but at the same time not without a hint that a certain improvised expurgation was operative as he talked.

'I suppose,' Penelope asked as she did finish her champagne, 'that he was the sort of person—eminent as a writer, I mean—whose life will have to be written by somebody?'

'It's sure to be. I'd say there are bound to be two or three books before the world begins to forget about Fulke Ferneydale.'

'Does this business of going through his papers hitch on to that? Is there stuff that will have to be suppressed, at least for the present, before the papers are made available for research?'

These acute questions, which were perhaps the fruit of Penelope's study of English literature at Oxford, visibly impressed Bernie as entirely relevant.

'I just don't know,' he said. 'I've never seen much of the stuff, which is all up in Fulke's work-room in the attics. But I don't think you and I are expected to work as censors. And it's my guess that we're not likely to come on anything much in the way of autobiography, or materials for a memoir. It's likely all to be working stuff: note-books and stray observations, and abortive starts on plays and novels. There were several such miscarriages and pseudo-pregnancies during the comparatively short time I was with him. I don't know that you're going to find it particularly interesting, or that it's quite your sort of thing—or mine either, for that matter. I think that if we just sort things into categories our duty will be done. After that, you'll simply have to discover the appropriate chaps to hand it all to. Or nearly all to. For processing, you know, before it's shoved profitably into print.'

'I still find it rather puzzling.'

'Yes, it is in a way. And—do you know?—I think we should put it all off for a little. You're entitled to be much more interested in the house and the countryside than in that particular chore. Or in me, for that matter. And that brings me to a first suggestion. It's that I take myself off for a few days—I've friends in Le Bugue I rather want to visit—and that then I come back—supposing, that is, you want me to—and that we get through the job as briskly as we can. Old Mme Saval isn't all that bright, but she'll be able to answer any questions of a practical sort. Sit on the terrace and absorb the view. Like the house, it's your very own, because there's nowhere else from which just *that* view is to be had. And André, circling the place on his little motor-mower, makes a kind of mobile *repoussoir* to the scene.'

Penelope felt that dinner had produced a rather different Bernie Huffer from the one she had first and briefly encountered. It might almost be said that decorum had been the key-note of the meal. And both his proposal to take himself off for a time and his disposition to deal lightly with Fulke's whimsical notion of an archivist or literary executor seemed to be considerate gestures. Yet, curiously enough, she wasn't altogether grateful. Perhaps Bernie had simply decided that she was an unpromising female from some undivulged point of view of his own, and that at Le Bugue—wherever that might be—lay metal more attractive. And he wasn't particularly looking forward to being associated with her in the hunt through what she was coming to think of as Fulke's lumber-room.

Having these last thoughts passing through her mind didn't please Penelope at all. They belonged, she told herself, to a green girl. But then she reflected that if she had turned up, as she expected to do, at an entirely deserted Le Colombier, she might have been conscious of her adventure as essentially a lonely affair. So she received Bernie's proposals with a good grace, and closed the door behind him almost with regret when he took himself off to his dovecot again at a fairly early, and therefore seemly, hour. Not, on the other hand, that he had bolted as quickly as he decently could. He had lingered to stack the dishes considerately for Mme Saval in the morning, and had given Penelope herself various pieces of information about what was where and how you coped with this or that. And he had said good-night with a touch of warmth but also with the deference of a well brought up boy to an older person. But this brought Penelope's thoughts—or feelings—full circle, and again she wasn't too pleased. To escape from the slight discomposure accompanying such unstable behaviour she made a short tour of the house before going to bed. Besides the Modigliani there was a Mondrian and a Picasso and a spindly Giacometti bronze—and probably in Fulke's upstairs work-room, which was locked and to which she found herself without a key, there would be further things of the same sort. She had never in her life seen such treasures except in public galleries, and the progressive sense of owning a museum was almost as disquieting as having inherited a secretary. When she went to bed, however, she fell asleep at once.

Mme Saval turned up while Penelope was still finding herself breakfast, and proved to be already aware that the new proprietor of Le Colombier had arrived. In fact she had brought a gift in the form of a couple of *croissants*, and she stood by as if to make sure that her English *patronne* consumed these luxuries with due appreciation. She seemed to be a very old woman, but this may have been the effect of a contorted frame and generally weather-beaten appearance which spoke of long habituation to the life of the fields. It was clearly her intention to be copiously informative, but her volubility and dialect were alike such that Penelope was left groping for her meaning more often than not. She had a good deal to say about the villa's late owner, venturing confidently into literary criticism with a vehement pronouncement that he had been *le plus grand écrivain anglais de ces derniers temps*. And she had a good deal to say about Bernie as well, but to an even less intelligible effect. The words *filles* and *fillettes* kept cropping up, however, sufficiently often to suggest that the young man was not particularly addicted to a monastic sort of life at Le Colombier. But was it Bernie who was mad about the girls, or the girls who were mad about Bernie? Perhaps, Penelope thought, what she was being told about was a rapid series of reciprocal attachments. But Bernie's love-life wasn't—couldn't conceivably be—any affair of hers, and in order to escape from Mme Saval (who disturbingly accompanied her conversation with a vigorous manoeuvring of various primitive sweeping and dusting implements) she offered a firm remark on the beauty of the morning and went out to the terrace, there to survey what Bernie had declared to be her very own view.

This proved to be not quite true. She was sharing the prospect, if from a very different angle, with two black kites, whose slow wheeling over what they must be jealously guarding as their sole territory was at once impressive and obscurely ominous. They were patiently waiting, Penelope thought, for a rendezvous if not with anything living then with something dead.

'Hullo, Penelope. I hope you slept well.' Bernie had appeared suddenly beside her, so that she started slightly before turning to him. And this he observed. 'Sorry to have forgotten to blow that whistle,' he said. 'But I'm just off, and wanted to pass the time of day. I say! There's a bit of poetry about you. But not by me. William Morris, I rather think. With wide wing the fork-tailed restless kite sailed over her, hushing the twitter of the linnets near. I rather like poetry. Fulke didn't.'

'It certainly is very still. But perhaps there aren't any linnets to hush. The indigenous humans have shot and eaten them.'

'They prefer larks, as a matter of fact. A horrible people, don't you think? What about Mme Saval—didn't you find her horrible?'

'Not in the least. Only garrulous. But I fail to understand every second sentence she utters.'

'You have to get tuned in. Then you'll find her no end informative. Particularly about me, if you happen to be at all curious. But there I go again. Another silly quip.' Bernie had thrown back his head momentarily, so that his hair, which was fine and of the colour of ripe corn, stirred like ripe corn in a breeze. 'But at least I'm departing, as I said. And I'll be back on Friday, and we can start in on those papers—unless, of course, you've decided to have nothing to do with them. By the way, do take a prowl through the dovecot. I'd like to think of you as inspecting the lair of the monster. Good-bye! And don't let the kites depress you. They've been there ever since I have, and I look on them as tutelary spirits.' Bernie Huffer had taken two steps backward, rather as if quitting the presence of royalty, and from this position he offered a small and nervous-seeming gesture, at once friendly and diffident. Then he walked quickly away round a corner of the house, and the sound of a car being started made itself heard a minute later.

Penelope felt no disposition to be depressed by the kites. But she found, rather to her surprise, that she at least wasn't heartened by Bernie Huffer's departure. He could be seen as a frivolous or at least dilettante young man, and he had adopted from the first a familiarity of address which didn't quite meet with her notions of what was proper at the beginning of an acquaintance. But Bernie must be at least ten years younger than she was. That was half a generation, and a period in which manners might change substantially without being noted as doing so by somebody who had been living so retired and even provincial a life as herself. At least Bernie was civilized and apparently well-read; he had produced that dinner with no fuss or bother whatever; and his taking himself off for a few days while she independently felt her feet at Le Colombier had been something markedly considerate. Moreover Bernie was tactful. He hadn't asked her if she had read Fulke's letter—and as a matter of fact she had not. There it had been, on a bureau in what had plainly been intended as her bedroom—and she had been weak enough to defer what she knew might be a disturbing experience. That was bad. So now she went back to the house at once, secured the letter, and returned to the terrace to read it in the comfortable warmth of the morning sun.

Dear Penelope,

I hope that before you have opened this letter you have accepted Le Colombier, arrived there, looked around you, and like the place. I feel I owe you a small gift, and the house, together with whatever happens to be in it when I die (which is to be quite soon) is just that. There are several pictures and things which poor Sophie may be prompted to appropriate. This I exhort you to resist.

There is also a young man called Bernard Huffer, who wants to be a painter but is at present my secretary. I've given him several thousand pounds to cover him over the longish period it may take to get matters as I should wish at Le Colombier, and cope with a shocking lot of uncompleted scribblings. Please give him a hand.

You are yourself, after all, right at the top of my list of unachieved proposals, and I like to think of you as turning over, and perhaps reading, the rest. A codicil to my will gives you formal control of it all. But of course you can, at any stage you choose, instruct Bernie to hand the material over to the professionals who have yanked me through my not altogether satisfying literary career.

There may be people who tell you that all this is rather rum, and bears the impress of a sick man's vagary. Don't believe them. I am entirely, as the lawyers say, *compos mentis*, and know what I am about.

Yours affectionately,

FULKE

P.S. I hope, and believe the leeches would agree, that you are likely to be reading this letter at Le Colombier in early summer. If so, lay it down where you picked it up, go outside, and don't get so absorbed in our famous view that you fail to see, and count, the wild flowers. F.F.

So here at least, Penelope thought, was something she could do at once and without misgiving. Indeed, she had already begun to comply, since she was sitting on the terrace with the view before her—which was seductive enough. But between her and that broad prospect of cultivated land south of the Dordogne there lay first the boy André's close-shaven lawn and then that meadow-like expanse of longer grass sloping gently downwards to a belt of woodland lying beyond. Of the wild flowers on this terrain she had been aware on her arrival the day before; there were clumps of them immediately catching the eye, and others less obtrusive there must be in abundance awaiting discovery. Penelope knew her flowers and birds, since her stepmother (when still Mrs Martin) had held them in a rather old-fashioned regard as essential elements in a well brought up girl's education. And she now felt that she would be a good deal more at home with orchids and spurges than with her late brother-in-law's residual papers. Had Fulke known about her fondness for the simple pleasures of botany, so that the final injunction in his letter harboured some faint irony? It was very improbable, and could scarcely have come even momentarily into her head had she been of a perfectly easy mind about her strange acquisition. But at least the papers were going to wait until Bernie's return to Le Colombier, and meanwhile the flowers were in front of her. She crossed André's commonplace lawn to the longer grass besprent with them, and the first thing she came upon was a patch of yellow Rock-rose, pretending as usual to be buttercups. Next to these, all stalk and tiny flowers, was what she knew only as Treacle Mustard. Lizard Orchids, Bee Orchids, Yellow Wort, St John's Wort: Penelope realized that to obey Fulke's injunction would be to go on botanizing for hours. And this she might have addressed herself to had a woman's voice not suddenly spoken from behind her.

'So there you are, Penelope! I couldn't make head or tail of what that dirty old woman said as to your whereabouts. And there was no sign, even, of the impertinent young man.'

Penelope, who had been kneeling over a late-flowering patch of Spurge Laurel, stood up to find herself in the presence of Fulke's widow. There was no mistaking this abundant presence for other than the former Sophie Dix, although long years had passed since Penelope had set eyes on her. So Bernie's confident assertion that Sophie had been repelled for good was proving to be ill-founded.

'Hullo, Sophie! But where is Silvan?' Penelope made this inquiry by way of receiving an unwelcome intrusion with proper polite behaviour. But she had to wonder what she should do if, in Bernie's absence, another determined attempt was going to be made upon the Modigliani. She had remembered during the night something about the picture that made any demand for it peculiarly outrageous.

'I persuaded Silvan not to come. We came together—on business, you will understand—a few days ago, and Silvan treated your insufferable Mr Huffer rather roughly. I had to restrain him, as a matter of fact.'

'Indeed?' Penelope produced this brief response on a note of decently muted scepticism. 'If you have come about a painting by Modigliani I'm afraid I can't help you. And my own business, at the moment, is simply looking at the flowers. I've always wanted to own what might be called a wild garden. And now I do.'

'I don't question that. I don't question Fulke's foolish behaviour over this little house. But the pictures——'

'Look, Sophie—*Prunella vulgaris*. Or Self-heal. The popular names

163

are always the nicest, don't you think? And just at your feet is Soap-wort—although the learned call it *Saponaria*.' It was with perhaps a censurable levity that Penelope thus engaged in the activity (recalled from childhood) of showing a guest round the garden. 'But shall we have a cup of coffee? It's very pleasant on the terrace.'

'We will stick to business here where we are, if you don't mind.'

'Just as you wish, Sophie dear.' Penelope was far from displeased that her offer of modest hospitality had annoyed her visitor very much. And now the two Ferneydale widows were facing one another squarely on their flowery carpet. To the kites high above them they might have appeared to be a new species of rodent resolved to fight it out over a bone.

'*All* the pictures are mine,' Sophie said. 'Fulke expressly made me a present of them.'

'Walked in with them under his arm, do you mean? How very extraordinary!'

'Don't be foolish, Penelope. They were gifts made at various times.'

'That must have been very gratifying. But why are you so particularly keen on the Modigliani?'

'Because Silvan likes it. In fact, I have promised that he may have it in his rooms when he goes up to Cambridge.'

'How very odd.' And Penelope really did think it very odd. Modigliani's nude as a work of art was presumably of high quality, but its erotic interest stood surely very close to zero. A Renoir of a lady similarly posed might have been another matter. But what Silvan wanted was simply a naked woman—and that was that. 'And Fulke,' she asked, 'bought it for you long ago?'

'Yes, of course. It was soon after our marriage.' Sophie hesitated for a moment. 'I remember the occasion so clearly.'

'I'm afraid there must be some confusion, Sophie. Perhaps there were two Modiglianis. Because what you say can't be true of the one here at Le Colombier.'

'Just what do you mean?'

'Caspar never talked very much about his brother.'

'I'd suppose not. Caspar must have been very jealous of Fulke's success. But you're getting away from what we have to discuss.'

'Far from it. I think it was just that Fulke had ceased to be very much in Caspar's mind. But Caspar did once happen to tell me how his brother came to own a Modigliani. It was long before the price of such things became grotesquely high. When, in fact, they were both undergraduates at Oxford. Of course it is conceivable that it was for you he destined it. He'd probably already glimpsed you once or twice. But it wouldn't be a story, Sophie dear, that would go down very well in a court of law. Or so I'd judge.'

'I shall consult my solicitor.'

'That's a thoroughly good idea. He may save you from making a further fool of yourself.' Penelope felt a decent slight dismay as she heard herself come out with this brutal remark. Had she not concurred with Dora Quillinan's suggestion that one or two of the artistic treasures possibly harbouring in Fulke's French villa might gracefully be ceded to his widow? But Sophie, she now told herself, was an impossible person. Almost everything the woman had said was objectionable—including her aspersing Mme Saval as a dirty old woman, and (more particularly, perhaps) her describing Bernie as impertinent and insufferable. It was true that about Bernie she had initially harboured some such thoughts herself. But she was of quite a different opinion about him now.

'And meantime,' Sophie said, 'I am very sorry to gather that you are living in a totally indecorous manner cheek by jowl with that insolent young man. I never liked him. I seldom liked any of Fulke's secretaries. For such a great writer, Fulke was a singularly poor judge of men.'

'Was he, indeed?' Penelope considered this to have been a particularly stupid remark. 'I can't recall it's being recorded in that long obituary in *The Times*. But I suppose you were in a position to know. And please take a message to your son. It is simply that if he engages in any further smash-and-grab adventures here at Le Colombier I shall send for the police at once.'

And at this these two English gentlewomen parted. The kites, which had been narrowing their circle as if the altercation were exercising upon them some centripetal force, wheeled away on larger and yet larger arcs, sweeping alike over woodland and meadow and the quietly flowing Dordogne.

XIII

MADAME SAVAL HAD departed, presumably for the day. But Penelope, as she approached the house, saw that she was again not going to be quite alone. A boy who must be André had appeared, and was sweeping the terrace with the sort of broom popularly associated with air-borne witches in full flight. On this June day there were few if any fallen leaves to deal with, and André was doing little more than stir up an inconsiderable cloud of dust. In some similar fashion, Penelope remembered, would Tommy Elbrow behave at the vicarage when hoping to combine an appearance of virtuous activity with the pleasures of casual talk with a member of the household. Penelope, although preoccupied with her recent encounter, paused to have a word with this further retainer.

'*Bon jour, André,*' she said. '*Moi, je suis Madame Ferneydale. Vous avez travaillé depuis longtemps chez Le Colombier?*'

'Good morning, Madame. For one year I work here.'

'And have learnt English? That's very good, indeed.'

'It is the language—the second language—of the Dordogne. So many English buy so many houses in Dordogne. One works here, one works there, and always there is English to hear. For one year I am *garçon de salle*, and always I listen to what I hear.'

André, Penelope saw, was less appropriately described as a boy than as a youth—of sixteen, perhaps, or seventeen. She wondered why he had declined from the glories of being a waiter in a café or a hotel to his present position. He was dressed in that pale blue cotton or denim which, well before it had established itself internationally as the uniform of a young generation, had been the garb of a French peasantry for a very long time. André might be Mme Saval's grandson, although his appearance would not be likely to put the idea in one's head. He was fair-haired, of a clear complexion, bright-eyed, and with full lips permanently ready to part in a friendly and ingenuous smile. He had opted, perhaps, for an easy life for a time. At Le Colombier there was no doubt wood to cleave and cart, shrubs to trim and paths to weed as well as grass to mow and a terrace to keep tidy. But it scarcely seemed a full-time job, and it was possible that André turned up only on so many days a week. At the moment Penelope made no enquiry about this, and after a few more words went on into the house. But the thought came to her that Fulke, having made money almost on the grand scale, had perhaps been a notably generous employer. In his letter there was that casually dropped 'several thousand pounds' as the sum left with Bernie Huffer to cover such residual activities as he was going to perform. At Mallows, whether in the vicarage or the Hall, 'several thousand pounds' would be quite something. And this made Penelope feel again that as one of her late brother-in-law's legatees she was on the fringes of a world of affluence alien to anything she knew. But at least about Le Colombier itself there was nothing showy—if one excepted, that was to say, half a dozen or a dozen objects in what might be called the Cézanne bracket, commercially regarded. She realized the ownership of these things was going to trouble her increasingly as out of scale with everything familiar in her life. She even wondered why she hadn't simply told Sophie to send a truck to take them away. Partly it had been that she supposed the transfer of such costly gifts to be not without complications of a legal sort. But much more, she had to confess to herself, it was because she had never greatly cared for Sophie Dix, and somehow had cared even less for Sophie Ferneydale. Having owned up to this in the small court of her own conscience, she set about contentedly finding herself a midday meal.

But the afternoon presented a problem she had been quite aware of as likely to keep turning up. Here she was, a young English widow, transported to a scene with which her sole connection was that of a legal ownership arbitrarily imposed on her by the will, or whim, of a man she hadn't seen for years; of a man, indeed, to whom her last remembered utterance had been a monosyllabic 'No.' It was true that Fulke Ferneydale, whose talents had earned him riches, could be seen as having done no more than his duty in making a generous bequest to his brother's widow. The second Mrs Henry Rich, who had herself been a widow left in circumstances so narrow that she had been obliged to become a professional governess over a substantial period of years, had been right in insisting upon the propriety of Fulke's behaviour. Nevertheless the form of his gift, and the unexpected obligation by which—although without legal force—it had proved to be accompanied, had landed her in what she was bound to feel as a deracinated condition. It might be true, as André had declared, that the Dordogne was stuffing with leisured English people, and that she might eventually find some society among these. Le Colombier itself she did feel she might come to love. But it would be only an idle sort of life that she could create there. It would be a life, surely, devoid of duties—and she had been brought up to feel, with Wordsworth, that Duty was the stern daughter of the voice of God. It had never, perhaps, been uttered to her in that magniloquent way, but at least she had been taught to put her back into the daily round and common task. As she washed up a single plate and a single knife and fork it came to her suddenly and clearly that Le Colombier was going to be no more than an episode in her life.

Penelope was taking a walk through the woods—probably her own woods—when the fact came back to her with renewed force. This time it was so incontrovertible that she wondered why it had not come to her sooner than it had done. The answer to this, she told herself in an almost alarming moment, might be Bernie Huffer. She had walked into a house of her own, something hitherto quite foreign to her experience, and there had been a young man, alien in the same degree, but almost instantly interesting and attractive on the very score of this fact.

Rationally viewed, there didn't seem a great deal to be said for Bernie. He had revealed himself as having no high regard for the genius of his late employer, and his own ambition didn't even lie in the field of literature. A seriously dedicated young painter, Penelope believed, would not have opted for a certain amount of security at the expense of the distracting business of being secretary to a popular and quirky author.

Still, Bernie Huffer was fun—and thus commanded something which Penelope was conscious of as having been in rather short supply for a good many years past. Her acquaintance with him had been of only a few hours' duration; yet she was actually missing him now. She wished she had brought Dora Quillinan as a companion on this exploration of her unexpected inheritance. Or did she? Hadn't she spoken truly when she had said to Dora that she wanted nobody nudging her in one direction or the other when she came to make up her mind about Le Colombier? Of course that resolution must be taken to cover Bernie Huffer, too, however amusing she found him. He was young and therefore probably callow; he knew next to nothing about her; once Fulke's papers were tidied up he would depart and she would never see him again. Bernie was no sort of factor in any decision she might have to make.

During these ruminations Penelope had wandered on without much regarding where she was going, and presently she awoke to the realization that she was lost. In the woodland through which she had been walking there was plenty of traversable ground between the trees, and she had seen nothing that could be distinguished as a path for some time. She couldn't, of course, be far from the villa, but even its general direction was unclear to her. Moreover she hadn't seen a soul during her wanderings, and even were she to do so there would be something absurd, she felt, in asking the way back to her own house. It might prove to be within a hundred yards of where she stood. So she walked on again at a venture. She must soon come either on a road or a glimpse of the great river in the valley below which would give her a chance of orienting herself. Meanwhile, her solitude was agreeably romantic. What she might meet was a hermit or a pilgrim (who would really be a magician in disguise), or even a knight in armour who would warn her of the vicinity of an obnoxious dragon. These excessively childish fancies were in her head when the trees thinned out before her and she found that she was looking at that *colombier* from which her house took its name. The house itself, however, was only just to be glimpsed through a further screen of trees.

Bernie, she remembered, had urged her to inspect 'the lair of the monster'—which was another piece of nonsense out of romance. It had been, all the same, a genuine injunction, and she told herself that he would be pleased to learn that she had complied with it. Moreover, she was curious about the young man's manner of providing for himself. So she walked up to the dovecot, found its single door casually ajar, pushed it open, and entered this odd abode.

A dovecot is normally a sort of high-rise dwelling into which a very numerous population can be crammed. But now, under a low ceiling, was a single apartment which afforded a considerable sense of space, even although the walls had been left pitted appropriately for their former inhabitants. In its centre rose a modern and elegant spiral staircase, giving access to perhaps more than one chamber above. And what was immediately revealed to her was at once a living-room and a studio. But the lighting seemed not very suitable for the latter purpose, which was perhaps why, when he betook himself to pigments, Bernie seemed to have formed that habit of working in the main sitting-room of the villa. One segment of the ancient structure was adequately fitted up as a kitchen, and what furniture there was in the rest was of a simple sort well-adapted to bachelor ease. There weren't many books, and there were no pictures on the walls, although a good many canvasses, some of them still virgin on their stretchers, were stacked up against them here and there. But on several tables, and even scattered carelessly on the floor, were numerous sketches in a variety of media—the favourite appearing to be pencil on damp paper. Without exception, they were of female nudes.

Penelope found herself studying some of these evidences of Bernie Huffer's industry with care. In two or three cases as many as half-a-dozen sketches displayed the same figure in slightly varying forms of the same pose. The effect was of a considerable tenacity and seriousness of intention in the artist. And artists, she believed, don't commonly produce that sort of thing straight out of their heads. They work from the life. Penelope wondered where the models came from. Presumably it was from the local rural populace. And this fact might explain Mme Saval's not very well understood talk about *filles* and *fillettes*.

These thoughts signalled to Penelope that her interest in this unfamiliar place was not a matter wholly of aesthetic consideration. She felt suddenly an intruder—and a disconcerted intruder at that. So she took herself out of the lair of the monster at once, closing its door behind her. She closed it, in fact, with a bang. For she was somehow displeased with Bernie for having suggested an exploration of what seemed to her to be an almost obsessive interest in female anatomy. Returning to the villa, she made herself a cup of tea provided *en mousseline* by Messrs Jacksons of Piccadilly. Her reaction to Bernie's labours was philistine, no doubt. But it was strong in her, all the same.

*

And in the course of the next few days several young women—all local peasant girls—turned up at Le Colombier, boldly rang the big bell at the front door, and were clearly disconcerted by the appearance of an unknown and presumably unsuspected English woman instead of the late owner's secretary. Two of them ventured upon speech, and were answered by Penelope in as matter-of-fact a fashion as she could contrive. Two others, who came together, merely turned to one another giggling, and then still giggling ran away. Penelope found herself particularly offended by the fact that none of these female visitors was particularly good-looking—or none in the conventional sense in which good-looks are judged by what is visible above the neck. But all were in other respects detectably personable. So it could be charitably assumed that their call was in a professional capacity as artists' models, and that they could thus be linked with the sketches so freely on display in Bernie's dovecot. Penelope knew very little about the habits of artists, but had a notion that as soon as they got a young woman stripped and perched on some sort of platform before them anything in the nature of an erotic response to the spectacle thus afforded banished itself in the interest of aesthetic feeling. But what about before and after? And what was the inference to be drawn from that unintelligible chatter of Mme Saval's on the subject of *filles* and *fillettes*? Penelope caught herself once or twice as lingering over these speculations; and she magnified this curiosity, inevitable and harmless in itself, into a charge of being very improperly obsessed by it. Was it conceivable that a primitive jealousy was at work in her? The mere possibility of this made her feel that she had come a long way from respectably resigned widowhood in the vicarage of Mallows.

Then a further realization came to her. During the last few days she had fallen into the way of holding a good deal of casual talk with the only slightly more-than-adolescent André. This again was surely innocent enough. André's English was elementary but nevertheless useful. His French, unlike the old woman's, wasn't difficult to follow. During Bernie's absence he was the only person for miles around to whom she could talk at all. Yet little that he said was of any substantial interest in itself, and so this attractiveness—which wasn't in the least overmastering—had to be viewed as of a very simple girl-and-boy order. This was comical rather than disconcerting. She had a memory of once having made a joke to Dora to the effect of her heart being touched by Tommy Elbrow when Tommy was much of André's age. But she wasn't a young girl now; she had for some time been habituating herself to the fact that middle age was looming well up on her horizon. So she oughtn't to be noticing that André owned one very simple sort of appeal more pronouncedly, perhaps, than the majority of boys of his age. The fact appeared to be that she had landed herself in an unwholesome near-solitude. She even began to feel that she would welcome Bernie Huffer's return from visiting his friends at Le Bugue.

And promptly on the Friday morning Bernie did turn up again. His car was heard on the drive; the engine stopped, a door banged, and his voice made itself audible round a corner of the house. He was shouting to André, cheerfully but imperiously, to come and wash the old crate down at once, since it was smothered in dust. The effect came to Penelope as that of a young squire in some Victorian fiction, confidently committing his horse to the attentions of a groom. Fleetingly, she wondered how much Bernie felt that he owned the place—with André and herself thrown in. But his manner as he joined her on the terrace, although remaining cheerful, became decently tinged with deference at once.

'Well, now you know, Penelope,' he said. 'You've had Le Colombier to yourself for a bit, and made up your mind about it. Are you going to like it? That's the grand question. And I've no doubt that Fulke in the shades is waiting anxiously to hear your reply.'

'I can give only a provisional one, so far.' Penelope had somehow not liked this particular fancy. 'It's rather unconnected with anything I've ever known, you see. I have a sense of this terrace as a stage, and the house behind it as an elaborate piece of stage carpentry. There ought to be a cast of not more than half-a-dozen people, entering and exiting through these various french windows, and building up rather a trivial leisure-class comedy.'

'In other words, a typical Fulke Ferneydale effort. Have you seen many of his plays, or read many of the novels?'

'None at all, as a matter of fact.'

'Hush, hush, for heaven's sake! Remember who's listening.'

Penelope failed to look amused, since she disliked Bernie's keeping up this particular joke. And it struck her that what she had revealed in so matter-of-fact a tone was really rather odd—particularly as coming from one who had been appointed to turn over the late playwright and novelist's literary remains. Why had it never so much as occurred to her to get one of Fulke's books out of the county library, which sent a van full of contemporary literature to park on the village green at Mallows every week? Why had Caspar never so much as suggested her taking a look at this or that, nor—so far as she could remember—kept anything of his brother's on his own shelves? Bernie must judge the Mallows Ferneydales and Riches an uncommonly provincial crowd. Penelope had, in fact, read a good deal, but mainly in those earlier fields of literature with which she had become familiar at Oxford at a time when that University had officially regarded the entire book-making industry as having come to a stop with the death of George Meredith in 1909.

'What enchanting news!' she now heard Bernie saying. 'You come with an absolutely virgin mind to that odd job of ours. Have you taken a dekko at any of those papers yet?'

'I haven't had the chance, so far as I can see. I assume they are all locked up in what must be rather a big room upstairs, which I don't seem to have the key to.'

'Stupid of me—and I'm so sorry. The key's in my pocket now. The Cézanne's up there, you know, and worth a huge fortune on its own. And the Sophie and Silvan affair turned me very security-minded.'

'Sophie's been here again, so I haven't been entirely on my own. But she wasn't interested in papers. It was just the Modigliani again. She feels that her son ought to have it for his rooms in Cambridge.'

'I don't believe that young lout will ever see Cambridge. I hope you were firm about it.'

'I was—very. I may even have been rather rude. The woman is Fulke's widow, after all.'

'And had to put up with a great deal, no doubt.' Bernie seemed to regret this graceless speech even as he uttered it. 'But I don't hold much of a brief for Sophie. Pots of money, and never done an honest day's work in her life. Not that there isn't a great deal to be said for money—particularly when you're inconveniently quite without it.'

Penelope almost said that Bernie couldn't be in that position now, since he had not so long ago had several thousand pounds from his late employer. But it was probably true that nobody much wanted to buy his pictures, and that penury had taken a peep at him early in his career. There seemed, indeed, no other explanation of his accepting such a blind-alley job as that of secretary to a popular writer.

'I think,' she said, 'that we ought to begin taking a look at those papers this afternoon. And I feel that quite a brief survey of them will tell me that I'm unlikely to be of any use at all about them.' Penelope said this with a good deal of conviction. 'Have you started doing anything about them yourself?'

'I've calendared them in a rough and ready way. That means getting them into as much of a chronological order as seems possible. If Fulke is going to have some sort of posthumous vogue or permanent reputation—which seems unlikely to me—all that will come to be judged terribly important. Fortunately, you know, it's all typescript; there's scarcely a page of holograph anywhere, so far as I can see. And Fulke wrote a vile hand, so that painfully deciphering his false starts and abortive notions and great thoughts generally would be quite too awful for words. Not that there mayn't be plenty of clever writing here and there. Fulke was clever. I came to feel that more and more as I worked for him. It's not something it would occur to one to say about Tolstoy or any of the real swells.'

Penelope agreed that Fulke had been clever, but refrained from making Bernie's further assertion a subject of debate. Bernie was undoubtedly clever too, and perhaps owned higher endowments as well. This, she told herself, she was unfitted to judge—and still less was she competent to pronounce upon the value of this or that among Fulke's literary remains. She had a notion that Fulke at some stage of his career had been over-ambitious, going after a kind of excellence that was beyond his reach. Having acknowledged this to himself he had probably settled down to gratify the common reader, and his final quirky idea had been prompted by the just yet unflattering notion that his sister-in-law Penelope was exactly that. Penelope found that she didn't care for this rôle at all. The situation was artificial and absurd, and she must get out of it as best she could. She liked Le Colombier, and to a rather surprising degree she liked Bernie; yet she wasn't at all sure that at the back of her mind there didn't lurk a strong and simple impulse just to go home. All this was behind her next remark.

'What I'd like you to do,' she said firmly, 'is to sift through all those papers a bit ahead of me, and simply show me anything that you judge to be of consequence. I think that will be enough to fulfil any obligation I may be said to have been put under in accepting this house—and a sort of endowment, I gather, going along with it. It's the common sense of the thing, Bernie, and I don't feel that common sense often leads one far astray.'

'Then I'll start in this afternoon.' Bernie may have been amused, but his immediate attitude was cheerful and without fuss. Was he, perhaps, too ready to acquiesce in any course of life that came his way? Wouldn't he be more worthily employed if, instead of accepting a good deal of money to mess around with Fulke's papers, he had called it a day so far as secretarial labour was concerned, and set himself up in some garret of a studio to wrestle with his own proper art? It was in Penelope's nature to take satisfaction in the spectacle of people seriously employed to the limit of their capacities. So she felt that possibly she even had a duty to encourage Bernie to see things that way. He was still very young, certainly much younger than herself, and this made the dash of frivolity one could distinguish in him harmless and rather fun. Her own association with him was going to be quite transient. Perhaps she could give him a bit of a lead, all the same.

'Yes,' she said. 'Let's go briskly to work, and get it all out of the way. I'm sure there are other things you want to get back to, Bernie.'

'Ring down the curtain, you mean, on this small comedy. Life is real! Life is earnest! Longfellow.'

So Bernie, who was quick to detect a train of thought, was laughing at her with a frankness that was part of his appeal. And Penelope—at least for the time—didn't mind this a bit.

Nor did she mind his again preparing a meal that evening, although the fact of its being a second occasion of the sort carried with it an odd suggestion of domesticity. The very easiness of Bernie's address enhanced this; they might have been a couple long habituated to just such a routine. But at least Bernie's talk didn't incline to the over-intimate. What he had to say referred mostly to his investigations of the afternoon.

'There's quite a lot of what they call juvenilia for a start,' he said. 'One piece is amusing—or at least it's an amusing idea. Shelley and Jane Austen. They're having an Imaginary Conversation.'

'Like in Landor?'

'Yes. There was a vogue for such things on the radio, it seems, a good long time ago. Shelley and Miss Austen are alone in the inside of a stage coach. Shelley's still at Eton, and he's hugging what Miss Austen takes to be a tuck-box. But it's really an infernal machine, which Shelley is preparing to loose off against the tyrants of the earth. It's rather a nice situation or confrontation. Only Fulke seems to have been unable to think of anything for them to say to one another. It's one of his earliest false starts. He may have written it while he was still at school himself.' Bernie got to his feet in order to pour Penelope a glass of his late employer's claret. 'Then there's an affair, almost equally abortive, which I'd date during his undergraduate days. It gets a little further, but I don't know that you'd care for it. Two tarts—one a high-class courtesan and the other a drab—find themselves most improbably stranded together in the waiting-room of some deserted railway station here in France. They square up to one another a little, and then—more improbably still—a young Englishman strays in on them. Again there's no development. But the piece is interesting, I suppose, as illustrating what was often going to be Fulke's way of setting up a situation and just trusting that something would come of it.'

'I'd imagine writers quite often go to work in that way.' As she said this, Penelope seemed to recall having herself as a small girl embarked on the composition of fairy stories much after the same fashion.

'Probably they do—and Fulke made quite a technique of it. It seems wasteful to me, just like embarking on a painting without having formed an overall design. If I was going to write a novel or a play, I wouldn't put a word on paper until I'd thought of some single and completed action which was to be the substance of the thing.'

Bernie Huffer wasn't only clever; judging by this Aristotelian pronouncement one had to credit him with being well-read too. Penelope felt that it would be a mistake to begin admiring Bernie. But he was at least a good deal more lively and attractive than, say, the majority of her father's parishioners.

On the day following his return to the villa Bernie embarked upon a routine which might have been based on a tactful feeling that he ought not to impose too much of his society upon his new employer. Every morning, and while Penelope was for the most part exploring the region in which she had now become almost a landed proprietor, he worked alone in Fulke's big library-room upstairs, sifting through a substantial batch of papers and singling out whatever he judged Penelope might like to see. The result was commonly of no great bulk, and he handed it over to her at lunch-time so that she might occupy herself with it for as much as she cared of the afternoon. Having thus, as it were, decently earned his keep, he retreated to his dovecot until the evening, and there presumably pursued his own proper artistic activities. Penelope approved of this programme. Whether or not the young man was going to turn out to be any sort of considerable painter she was without the competence to determine. But it was right that he should stick to the attempt. Being an artist must be vastly more rewarding than burrowing however effectively in a deceased author's scrap-books.

Penelope could see, however, that the scrap-books and fugitive papers were not without interest at times. Fulke appeared to have done his thinking on a typewriter, and to have let his mind wander from one project to another with scarcely a pause in the clicking of the keys. Then periodically he would disengage the various fragments of something judged promising from their random context, and build up a more substantial synopsis of a play or novel with the help of scissors and paste. But since Penelope's knowledge of his achieved works was so culpably non-existent she had no idea whatever of what, amid all this disorder, might be leading where. Fulke could not, of course, have foreseen this total incapacity on his sister-in-law's part. As things were, she was without the means of determining the relative interest or importance of one fragment or another—although Bernie, presumably, would be able to do so. Those red-headed men in the Sherlock Holmes story who were set the task of copying out the *Encyclopaedia Britannica* were not more uselessly employed than was Penelope in thumbing through Fulke Ferneydale's notes and jottings. It was possible, no doubt, that some completed or nearly-completed works might turn up later—in which case she could stand in as the Common Reader he had appeared to envisage. Penelope had a mounting sense, however, that she was involved in an absurdity.

So, not unnaturally, her attention frequently strayed away from the typescript before her. She told herself how much more sensibly Bernie Huffer was employed in his dovecot, pencil in hand and paper before him—and perhaps before him, also, one (or conceivably two) of those giggling peasant girls. The image thus formed in Penelope's mind gave her no pleasure; was, in fact, disturbing as well as indelicate. But it continued at times to come between her and the typescript page.

Then an afternoon turned up on which she frankly declared to herself that she was not a bond-slave to Fulke and his remains. If she preferred to all these *disjecta membra* another stroll under a marvellous June sky she was perfectly free to put in time that way. So she pushed aside her papers, and within a few minutes was wandering through the woods. By this time she had discovered how to preserve a general sense of her direction as she walked. Every now and then there was a glade, and in any of these she had only to pause and look overhead. For there would be the black kites, sweeping in their effortless arcs in what she knew to be the southern quarter of the sky. But in addition to this there were now individual trees that were familiar to her, just as there were in the spinneys and copses for several miles round Mallows vicarage. It thus came about that when she eventually made a certain change of direction it was with the full knowledge that she was now—as once before—approaching Le Colombier *du coté de chez Huffer*. Within minutes the *colombier* would be squarely before her. She was at least too honest with herself to treat this as a surprise. Indeed, she told herself that she was being idly overcome by feminine curiosity. Yet, after all, why not pay Bernie an afternoon call? It could be regarded as a sign that she was prompted to take a friendly interest in his more serious activities.

With this in her head, and while approaching the dovecot from the rear, she became aware of something that might well have made her hesitate. There was here a window on the ground floor, too high for any observation from without, but now standing open to the afternoon sun. And through it there came sounds not readily to be identified with any serious artistic pursuit: sounds of panting, slapping, and low sharp laughter, which were at least sufficiently explicable to tell Penelope that were she to persist in her notion of an afternoon call a considerable degree of embarrassment might ensue. But when she had half-achieved this change of plan, and the door of the dovecot was in consequence in view, it burst open and André tumbled through. Flushed and laughing, he took in Penelope at a glance, and then bolted round the building like a rabbit making for its burrow. He was buttoning up what clothing he wore as he ran.

Penelope, if surprised, felt relieved as well. She had to acknowledge to herself how much she had disliked the idea of Bernie at work upon those young women. But this afternoon, at least, he had opted for a male model, and André had been conveniently to hand. She had herself arrived when the session had ended in some piece of skylarking of a decidedly juvenile sort. She would tease Bernie about this at dinner that evening.

But in fact she did not. What made her refrain she didn't clearly know. She was aware only of a new and disturbing image of Bernie Huffer somewhere upon the borders of her mind.

Part Five

XIV

'WE HAVE HAD a letter from Penelope.'

Mrs Rich gave this information to Charles Gaston upon his arrival at the vicarage on what had turned into a routine weekly call on its incumbent. Mr Rich was rapidly becoming a valetudinarian, accumulating small anxieties at a rate requiring regular reassurance that all was fundamentally as it should be in a man of advancing years.

'A most amusing letter,' Mrs Rich went on. 'As you know, Penelope went off a fortnight ago to inspect her surprising French inheritance. She finds Le Colombier to be quite enchanting.'

'I'm delighted to hear it.' Gaston, who had long suspected Mrs Rich of having divined his feelings about her stepdaughter, was careful to give no particular emphasis to this reply.

'But there is something a little out of the way, as well. Entering what she believed to be an untenanted house, she found herself in the presence of a young Englishman, engaged upon some sort of abstract painting. It was, Penelope says, like a small *coup de théâtre*. There is something slightly odd in the mere phrase.'

'Fulke was a man of the theatre. Penelope may have been thinking of that.'

'Very true. Well, the young man turned out to have been Fulke's secretary, and to be named Bernie Huffer. He made a little joke to the effect that he "went with the house". Fulke, it seems, had arranged that this Mr Huffer should remain at the villa for a time, to help Penelope with sorting through his papers. It seems to me'—Mrs Rich paused for a moment, and in a manner somehow reminding Gaston that here was Mrs Martin still—'just a little bit strange.'

'Do you mean not quite proper?'

'There is an old woman who comes in to wash up and tidy round, and there is a boy who cuts the grass.' Mrs Rich paused again on this oblique reply. 'And Mr Huffer is quartered not in the house itself, but in the dovecot, where he has established a studio.'

'You feel that to be reassuring?'

'I hope I feel no need to be reassured, or not in the obvious sense. Penelope is not a child.'

'That's certainly true.' Gaston reflected on the years he had let pass without venturing on a second proposal to Penelope in her widowed state. 'And she doesn't, I take it, describe this Bernie as being as enchanting as the villa?'

'She appears to find him very entertaining. It is something we haven't much gone in for at the vicarage.'

'Will she be entertained by Fulke's literary remains? I suppose that's what is meant by his papers.'

'I gather that there was a letter from Fulke awaiting her at Le Colombier. If it expressed some sort of wish that she should concern herself with the matter, she might feel that the task, like Mr Huffer, went with the house.'

'It seems an odd idea to me.' Gaston sounded really puzzled. 'Penelope is fond of poetry, but has no consuming interest in present-day literature as a whole.'

'I agree with you. But Penelope is bound to be conscious that Fulke has treated her, as Caspar's widow, handsomely enough. Nevertheless there is certainly something unseemly, or at least unfortunately contrived, in her being put into double harness with a strange young man. I admit to hoping that she will herself see it as that, and lose not too much time in sending Mr Huffer about his business.'

'I must go about mine.' Gaston made a gesture in the direction of Mr Rich's study. 'What does her father think of it all?'

'He has expressed no more than his belief that there is a respectable family of Huffers in Northumberland, although they are of German origin and keep an extra "e" in the name—like that writer, I suppose, who ended up as Ford Madox Ford. But my husband may have more disturbing thoughts as well. I have tried not to arouse alarm, and am sure you will do so, too.'

Dr Gaston found little to say in a professional way to his patient, or at least little that was new. But he felt that, as a friend of the family, he was bound to make some reference to the news that had come from

France. So on this topic he embarked, although keeping Mrs Rich's admonition well in mind.

'I'm delighted,' he said, 'to learn that you have heard from Penelope, and that she seems to find her new possession very much to her taste.'

'And her new companion, too. I can scarcely be said to understand the situation at all. Fulke Ferneydale acted very properly in doing something substantial for his brother's widow—and the more so because poor Caspar seems never to have been able to put together sixpence of his own. But so to arrange matters as to provide her, into the bargain, with a young male associate in what appears to be a singularly isolated dwelling strikes me as being, to put it mildly, misconceived.'

'But—as your wife has just been saying to me—Penelope is not an inexperienced girl. I don't think you need have any cause for alarm.' As he said this, Gaston realized that he mustn't continue fibbing—and indeed that the vicar was already, so to speak, too surprisingly on the ball to make fibbing feasible. 'Or for any *immediate* cause for alarm,' he emended. 'Penelope has behind her a sound education and a strong family tradition of right conduct in serious affairs. If this young man offends her sense of what is proper, she is likely to give him his marching orders at once. If I understand the thing aright, she is virtually his employer. It lies within her power to sack him on the spot.'

'There is truth in what you say, Gaston. But you might well add to your sketch of my daughter that, through one reason and another, she has moved into her thirties a little short of experience in the broader sense of the term. Caspar, although I had a high respect for him, seems unlikely to have been a very exciting man to marry. It is a point we do well to bear in mind. To be quite frank with you, her continued widowhood over a substantial stretch of time has been something of a disappointment to me.'

Not unnaturally, these cogent remarks from one who was commonly no more than a fretful old man held Gaston for some moments dumb, so that it was the vicar who continued the conversation still.

'We rightly acknowledge to our Creator that a thousand ages in his sight are like an evening gone. But profane literature has its lessons to. *Eheu fugaces, Postume, Postume, labuntur anni.* I am frequently conscious that my own life reflects something of what Horace intends.'

'We have all in our time let opportunities slip, no doubt.' Gaston paused for a moment before adding anything to this commonplace (but, as it happened, deeply felt) remark. Henry Rich presumably had behind him—if very far behind him—an acquaintance not only with Horace but with Catullus and Martial too. Or he must at least possess a bookish knowledge of some of the vagaries of sex. 'But there is another point, if not a very pleasant one, which we have to bear in mind. This Bernie Huffer appears to have been the latest of Fulke Ferneydale's secretaries. And I happen to have assured knowledge that they were all very good-looking young men.'

'And catamites to boot, no doubt.' The Reverend Mr Rich came out with this quite astoundingly in his stride. 'But that may not greatly mend matters. On the contrary, Gaston. There are homosexual men who derive satisfaction from having women fall in love with them. There are also men who are attracted by one sex or the other according to what turns up. I imagine that to have been true of Fulke Ferneydale himself. Was it not so?'

'It was so, or approximately so. You simplify a little, but on the broad facts of the case I possess, as it happens, quite conclusive information. It was a matter of Fulke having made me, for a time, something of a confidant. And the situation *does* become alarming'— here Gaston cast Mrs Rich's admonition to the winds—'if it holds true of this Bernie Huffer as well. That Penelope should become even a little attached to such a person would be very unfortunate indeed.'

'Have you a reliable locum, Gaston?'

'I beg your pardon?'

'A reliable locum.'

'Certainly I have. A retired man, always willing to lend a hand.'

'Then get into an aeroplane—they go all over the place nowadays—and find out how the land does lie.' Mr Rich paused as if considering the sufficiency of this. 'And then act as you can. My wife and I, let me say, are not without a sense of what you feel about my daughter.'

As Gaston drove back to his surgery he reflected in some anxiety on these two conversations. It was surprising that old Henry Rich, despite all his hypochondria and his twaddle about the Problem of Time, had thought to better purpose over Mr Bernie Huffer than had his capable and intelligent second wife. It was not conceivable that Mrs Rich had never heard of what Tommy Elbrow the gardener had termed Fulke Ferneydale's versatility: the breadth, as it might be called, of that celebrated author's erotic interests. But even confidentially to himself she had made no mention of this now—presumably because, Fulke being safely dead, his proclivities were without relevance to Penelope's present situation. But what did Penelope herself know? Here was an entirely open question. Caspar Ferneydale would certainly have deemed it proper to refrain from any communication to his wife of what he would undoubtedly regard as a reprehensible streak in his brother's character, and it might well be that Penelope had gathered only that Fulke possessed some untidy and unedifying sexual life. If Mrs Rich knew this to be the limit of her stepdaughter's knowledge she might decide to leave it at that, and might think of Bernie Huffer merely as a young man who, given the present set-up at Le Colombier, was likely to make a nuisance of himself after the fashion to which young men are always liable. But this was an inadequate view of the kind of risks that might be blowing around. Surprisingly, old Mr Rich had appeared to be as aware of them as Gaston was. But Gaston, in addition, felt that there lurked in the situation possibilities—even bizarre possibilities—which he himself was far from clear about.

And how was he going to act when he emerged from that aeroplane and found himself on French soil? He would, presumably, hire a car, and in it make his way to Le Colombier. But how, or as what, was he to present himself to the villa's new proprietor? He couldn't renew his acquaintance with Penelope Ferneydale amid a shower of lies designed to suggest that chance alone had brought him into her presence. He must appear all nakedly in the rôle of a knight errant—either as this or (what would be even worse) as the ambassador of an apprehensive and misdoubting parent. And in one or other of these guises he might prove to be blundering into a situation over which Penelope was entirely in control. The whole exploit might be simply a cooking of his own goose or a queering of his own pitch.

In fact Charles Gaston didn't like his own position at all, and he might have hesitated but for the knowledge that he liked Penelope's even less. As it was, immediately he was within reach of his telephone he rang up that useful locum, and then rang up Heathrow. It was then some further time before he realized how early his action had in fact been determined. A single phrase in Penelope's letter as it had been reported to him had made it inevitable that he should thus in haste set out.

XV

NOT, OF COURSE, that the *coup de théâtre*—or, at any rate, the major *coup de théâtre*—was likely as yet to have taken place. Gaston arrived at this perception just as his plane touched down at Bordeaux, and he did no more than cling on to it during the general fuss of going through passport control and customs and the business of finding his way to his waiting self-drive car. But as soon as he was clear of the air-terminal and with an open road ahead of him he fell to probing the state of affairs at Le Colombier with those words of Penelope's as a point of departure. She had expected solitude in the villa; instead of solitude there had been a young man; and this small surprise had carried with it at least a fleeting sense of the theatrical or contrived.

Whether this impression had remained with Penelope for long there was no means of determining, but at least she had described Bernie Huffer as entertaining, which suggested that she had accepted the unexpected set-up without undue alarm. The fact revealed something about the comportment, if not the underlying character, of the young man. Mr Huffer must own considerable address; he could have said or done nothing to displease; and he had been clever enough to distract Penelope's attention from the patently artificial nature of the entire situation. That Caspar's brother should have left her a villa in France made in itself—as everyone kept on saying—quite tolerable sense. But why had Huffer gone along with the place, and why had she been charged with the duty of there collaborating with him in sorting through a mass of papers? This was the point at which nonsense entered the picture—or if not nonsense then some malicious design.

Having got thus far in his thinking, Charles Gaston became aware that he was overtaking a good many cars larger and more powerful than his. So he eased up on the accelerator. It wasn't that he felt he must get to Le Colombier at a breakneck pace; on the contrary he knew that he required more time for thought, and that it was his own mental processes that he was attempting to speed up by injudicious pressure on the pedal. So he slowed down to a steady sixty kilometres an hour.

He had known a good deal about Fulke Ferneydale; had known him capable of *outré* behaviour in certain rather trivial but displeasing ways; had believed him to harbour resentments more readily than most men; and he had received from Caspar Ferneydale a strong impression that, very long ago, Fulke had wanted to marry Penelope and had proposed to her in vain.

And the whole situation, Gaston told himself, had to be considered within the context of Fulke's sexual proclivities—which might or might not be precisely mirrored in those of Bernie Huffer. The nub of the matter lay there, and it placed Huffer as an agent rather than a principal in what was going forward. And what was going forward could be nothing less than a fantastically conceived posthumous Ferneydale comedy.

Charles Gaston had done no more than a further five kilometres before deciding that the general mechanism of this comedy was clear to him. What wasn't so clear was the strategy he must adopt in face of it. And it would be unwise to arrive at the villa without some clearly formulated plan. So he decided to put up for the night at a nearby hotel and make his appearance at Le Colombier a fairly early-morning occasion. Penelope's extraordinary position—for it was certainly that—it would be prudent to sleep upon.

Gaston was not without misgivings as he put this resolution into effect. All the home-work that he could usefully do ought to have been done before he got off his plane, and there was surely irresolution in thus pausing to scratch his head for a night when within an hour's run of Penelope's dwelling. But in fact his delay, if censurable in itself, was to prove fortunate as actually accelerating the final stages of the affair. When he did reach Le Colombier it was to find that the dove—if Penelope might be so conceived—had flown. But only, indeed, with a day's packet of sandwiches under her wing.

'No, she isn't.' Bernie Huffer—as he clearly was—had appeared at the door of the villa hard upon Gaston's obeying the injunction, *Sonnez ici.* 'Mrs Ferneydale has gone off for a long walk, and I don't expect her back till early evening. I think she likes this part of the world, and is keen on getting to know it better. I haven't, in fact, seen much of her during the last few days. But I hope she's coming to like the house too.' The young man gave this information with a ready informativeness that sounded entirely friendly, and backed up this impression with an engaging smile. But Gaston felt something wary about him, all the same. Huffer was covertly disconcerted as an actor might be when confronted by a character who has come on stage to a totally unexpected cue.

'My name is Charles Gaston. I am Mrs Ferneydale's doctor, as it happens, but also a family friend.'

'And just passing through? I do hope you can wait until she gets back.'

'No, I'm not just passing through. I have business with Mrs Ferneydale—and I believe with you, too. Am I right in thinking that you are Mr Huffer?'

'Yes, you are. How odd that you should have heard of me! I hope you're not having to make what they call a domiciliary visit in the interest of Mrs Ferneydale's health?'

'We mustn't be frivolous, Mr Huffer. And, with your permission, I will come in for a short talk.'

'Oh, yes—do.' Bernie, as if some prudent counsel had now prevailed with him, swung the door wide and made a welcoming gesture as he did so. 'I've lived abroad a lot, you know, and it's always nice to hear a spot of the Queen's English.'

Gaston made no reply to this idle remark, but stepped into the hall and paused to look about him.

'Nothing changed, I see,' he said. 'Even the Modigliani hanging where it always hung. I occasionally felt there was something slightly odd—whimsical after Fulke Ferneydale's manner—about the lady being so placed as to greet you on entering the house.'

'You mean you've been here before?' Asking this, Bernie had failed to keep a certain sharpness out of his voice.

'Dear me, yes. Visiting Fulke and Sophie and Silvan. And a young secretary whose name I've forgotten. It was a little before your time, Mr Huffer.'

'Yes—and I don't think I ever heard your name mentioned, Dr Gaston. But of course Fulke had oceans of acquaintances. Come into the sitting-room, won't you? I do a bit of painting in it sometimes, by way of a change from my own quarters. They're in the *colombier*, as perhaps you've also heard.'

'Yes, indeed. Penelope has mentioned it in a letter to her father and step-mother. Among other things.'

'What about making you a cup of coffee?' As he spoke, the young man indicated a comfortable chair. 'I used to do house-maiding jobs for Fulke at a pinch, you know. And knowledgeable coffee-making was one of them.'

'Thank you, no. I breakfasted less than an hour ago.' Gaston, as he sat down, felt that he was beginning to know a little about Bernie Huffer. Bernie had sensed the presence of an enemy, and had to make an effort to be even momentarily polite. But this was done in a fashion suggesting that he could command considerable charm. And gaiety too, no doubt, so there was nothing surprising in Penelope's having found him an agreeable companion. That she could be in any danger of losing her head over him was a different proposition altogether. But some important questions about Fulke's former secretary were as yet unresolved. Bernie might now be what Fulke had been through a long phase of his career: a basically homosexual man who took pleasure in his ability to seduce and subjugate women. It was in this that Bernie may have been Fulke's pupil. Alternatively, Bernie might simply enjoy the *frisson* of having dangling after him one or another female who, sexually, meant nothing to him at all. Gaston was well instructed in the presence, throughout all human geography, of these and other meandering paths. What he found himself not bearing to believe in was the possibility of Penelope's becoming substantially involved with this equivocal young man. Even her being for a time lured into some painful absurdity was a horrible thought, and it was this that he feared as he took the measure of Bernie Huffer.

'Would you describe yourself,' Bernie asked easily, 'as having been a close friend of Fulke's at one time?'

'Not exactly that. But we were fairly intimate in a casual fashion, and he tended to confide in me over one thing or another.' It wasn't clear to Gaston whether Bernie had meant to import some innuendo into his question, and he was far from prompted to explain that his odd association with Fulke had indeed begun in a bad guess on Fulke's part. 'And to show off some of his side-lines. His photography, for example.'

'His photography?' Bernie had momentarily stiffened where he sat. 'Oh, yes—all that. He rather liked to obtrude it, didn't he? He'd confess that it was a childish hobby for a serious artist. But he was a complex chap. He'd say at times that his novels and plays weren't much more than photography. It was meant to sound like a kind of false modesty. But in fact it was pretty well the truth of the matter, as he clearly knew. And the existence of his betters wasn't the challenge it ought to have been; rather it was something very like an incubus. Fulke was an instance of the working of the inferiority complex— which was fashionable psychological jargon a long time ago.'

'You don't appear, Mr Huffer, to rate either your late employer's endowments or his character very highly.'

'Oh, well—he was extremely successful at his own true level. But I don't feel that he was unjustly denied the O.M. Do you?'

'Of course I don't. Surely it's odd, isn't it, that you should want to carry on as a sort of posthumous secretary to so mediocre a person?'

'There's money in it—in a short term way.' Bernie contrived to utter this avowal with an engaging ingenuousness. 'And the world is readier, you know, to do without pictures than it is to do without pills and potions.'

'And there's fun in it as well?' The sudden flash of insolence in Bernie's last remark had been felt by Gaston as marking definite progress. The young man's *insouciance* was wearing thin.

'Fun?' Bernie repeated with a little too much of whimsical surprise. 'I wouldn't call Le Colombier exactly a fun fair.'

'Then let me be more explicit.' Gaston paused for a moment on this, and in the pause it came to him that he was talking to a thoroughly conceited person. Bernie had that fondness for ridicule which often goes along with a marked distaste for being oneself exhibited in a ludicrous light. Briefly pondering this, Gaston felt that at last he saw his way ahead. 'Let me be more explicit,' he repeated, 'even at the risk of being a little too candid for your taste. Your self-regard is such that you can't resist any opportunity of being ever so clever—even if it is only as a puppet dangling from a dead man's strings. Or perhaps you see yourself as a kind of deputy puppet-master, obeying instructions to contrive a deft and nasty situation with Mrs Ferneydale at the centre of it.'

'I don't call that being candid; I call it being bloody rude. And I think that perhaps we'd better call it a day.'

'I've no wish to be gratuitously rude.' Gaston ignored the suggestion that this interview should be brought to a close. 'But I'm here to get a very displeasing mess cleared up. And I know just where to begin. You talked psychology a couple of minutes ago. Well, Fulke had a fondness for what he called experimental psychology, had he not?'

'Oh, all that.'

'And based a good deal of work on his conception of it. You set up a situation, a little nexus of personal relationships, and then you sit back and watch what happens. And if what happens is sufficiently discomfiting, or turns into a kind of black comedy, so much the better—whether it be either in real life or in fiction. And that's what we are in the first act of now. It just so happens that I am myself a wholly intrusive character—and Fulke, to do him justice, wouldn't have disapproved of me. If he's looking down on this precious spectacle now, I believe he's being rather pleased with it. The situation develops surprisingly, and that's the main thing.'

'Do relax, Doctor. Do relax if you have at all the trick of it.' Bernie's tone had fallen back upon impertinence. 'For I suppose you intend to stay until Penelope gets home in the evening, and pour out all this rubbish over again to her. And I rather think, you know, that you'll find she quite likes me.'

'Liking, perhaps. But continued believing is another matter. Were I to enter with her on the brisk sort of *exposé* I am adopting with you, and you were to deny it all, I judge it likely it would be me that she would see to be telling the truth. But of course I intend to do nothing of the sort.'

'You wouldn't dare to, you mean.'

'I mean nothing of the kind, young man. The whole sorry situation as I see it I will certainly communicate to her. But in my own time. Which means, among other things, after you leave Le Colombier.'

'But I'm not leaving Le Colombier. Aren't you taking a little too much for granted?'

'Listen to me a little longer. And let us go back to those photographs. To those two very special albums of them, that is. Do you know where they're hidden?'

'No, I don't.' Bernie checked himself. 'I don't know what you're talking about.'

'I could walk straight up to them now, but you yourself would have to pull the whole place to bits before you laid your hands on them. The situation's awkward for you, is it not? It was Fulke's streak of bravado that made him show them to me, almost in the presence of his wife and child. The first could already have been called the closed sequence, I imagine, since by that time Fulke had quite settled down as an admirer of young men. But here were his women, or at least a full dozen of them, all naked, and all posed as the *Venus dei Medici*. Coyly masking those parts that men delight to see. That's how some poet describes the pose.'

'Marlowe—but distinctly in another connection.' Bernie Huffer managed this piece of perkiness in something like desperation. For he was starting in horror at this unspeakable intruder upon a stage that he had believed himself wholly to command only half-an-hour before.

'The second album might have been described as the continuing series. It chronicled, if that's the word, Fulke's boy friends. Do you remember Rodin's *L'Age d'Airain?*'

'I don't know what on earth——'

'Come, Mr Huffer. Rodin's model, you know, was a young Belgian soldier who was a carpenter in civil life. And the bronze is so staggeringly realistic that everybody believed that the sculptor had cheated and taken moulds from the living man. But that's by the way. The pose is a very striking one—and rather disturbing, to my mind. But don't tell me you've forgotten stripping and taking it up for Fulke's camera. It's true that I admit an element of conjecture at this point. Your turn would have come several years after the last of the youths at that time commemorated in the album. When I saw it, it finished up with somebody called Cyril. Probably you haven't been the only boy-friend to go in after him. But I wouldn't really know. Fulke may have had his phases of fidelity.'

'Well, that's a little less cock-eyed than most of your notions.' Bernie had momentarily recovered his lightness of air. But at the same time he was scowling, which was perhaps his habit when he felt he was losing his bearings in a situation. 'And just where do we go from here?'

'I know where I'm heading, Mr Huffer. Just where you go when you leave Le Colombier is a matter of indifference to me. But leave it you shall.'

'I'll do nothing of the sort. And you have no title to be here at all. So it's you who had better clear out.'

'Let us try to be reasonable, Mr Huffer. Clearly, were I to show that second album to Mrs Ferneydale, your silly play would be over—but at the cost of a sudden and brutal shock to the lady. I want to avoid that. You can see that I want to avoid it, and that your only remaining bargaining point consists in just that. The album as a whole is perfectly publishable, you see. It couldn't even be stigmatized as outright pornographic. And it would give enormous amusement to everybody who knows you. There you'd be—tagging along in the dusty rear of a whole platoon of fancy boys. Have you a car here?'

'Of course I have.'

'Then pack up and take yourself off. You can send a van later to collect whatever you have to leave behind.'

'I suppose this is the point at which I say you win. But don't think I'd ardently set my heart on seeing the silly business through. I just thought it might be fun to bring it off.'

'Precisely. Your whole character is there in a nutshell. But I must know, by the way, just what the *dénouement* was going to be.'

'You never will—or not unless you first unearth those albums and hand them over to me.' Bernie was now doing his best to assume the manner of a cool negotiator. 'Is that agreed?'

'Decidedly not. But they shall be destroyed, undivulged, at the proper time.'

'Do you think I'm going to believe that?'

'Yes, I do, as it happens. It's plain to you that I'm endowed with common honesty, and in consequence a man of my word.'

'Oh, very well. It's not all that elaborate. I was to win my way into Penelope's affections, and then make her rather jealous through a bit of apparent philandering with the local girls. I've been working quite hard at that; I even contrived that she'd discover me to have been engaged on a series of sketches of the female form divine. She very nearly discovered something quite different about one of the local boys. But she was just too simple-minded to make it.' Bernie provided this last piece of information almost resentfully. 'So the play went on. You probably know we've been sorting through Fulke's papers.

Sketches for plays and novels and short stories: that sort of thing.'

'Well?'

'What was to turn up eventually, and be presented to Penelope, is the outline of a story in which a young English woman inherits a villa in France, and along with it—forgive my blushes, Doctor—an enchanting young man, who unfortunately turns out to be totally uninterested in——'

'I think that will do.' Gaston had stood up abruptly. 'But please understand one thing. Perhaps because of my profession, but I rather think just as a matter of temperament, I'm not at all bothered by the general spectacle of homosexual relationships and activities. They've existed since the beginning of time—and good luck to them. But a twisted-up performance such as Fulke has here devised and you have here been treacherously enacting is another matter. It may be said to be letting down the side.'

'Do you know, I think there's something in that last point?' As Bernie made this rejoinder he actually recovered his most engaging smile. 'But I'm quite glad it's all over—and off I'll go. But if I might just have those two albums to take with me——'

'Most certainly not. I repeat that you have my promise to destroy them in due season, and that must be enough. And now I am going for an hour's walk in those woods. When I return, you will have cleared out. Good morning.'

XVI

Gaston was away for a little more than an hour, and when he returned to the villa it was to find that Bernie Huffer had departed. Nor was there any sign of the old woman who came in to clean, so it could be assumed that she was taking a day off. But on the terrace a youth in patched blue jeans was engaged in the unexacting task of here and there hoeing out a weed from crevices in the stone surface. He straightened up as Gaston approached.

'André,' he said informatively, as he regarded the visitor with more interest than seemed required. 'You are Monsieur Bernie's new friend—yes?'

André was a good-looking boy, and gave Gaston the impression of going about with a permanent awareness of the fact. There was a certain impudence in the manner in which he had planted himself in the path of Mrs Ferneydale's unknown guest.

'Very new,' Gaston said shortly. 'I met him for the first time this morning.'

'But now Monsieur Bernie has driven away *dans sa voiture*, and with much bags: *quatre, cinq valises*. As on holidays.' André was clearly as proud of his English as of his well-favoured person. 'So you and I, monsieur, are now here alone.' The boy smiled brilliantly as he offered this uncontrovertible information. And he accompanied it with a slight gesture that was impudent indeed. Gaston, although he had so recently assured Bernie that he felt no sense of outrage before evidence of deviant behaviour, found this decidedly too much for him.

'*Allez-vous-en!*' he said brusquely.

'*Mais, monsieur——*'

'*Va-t'en, vite, André!*'

At this even less polite expression, André realized that he had been under a misconception about Monsieur Bernie's friend, and took himself off the terrace with satisfactory speed. Gaston went into the villa, glanced absently at the Modigliani, and then noticed on a low table in front of the picture, a scrap of paper written on in a bold hand. He picked it up and read:

> *Thou hast conquered, O pale Galilean!*
> So I have checked out.   B.H.

This final token of levity on Bernie's part Gaston crumpled and thrust in a pocket, before mounting the stairs to the large, low room in which it had been Fulke's habit to work. Except for the break of a couple of dormer windows, books went up to the ceiling on three sides of it. But the wall facing the door was bare except for a single painting. This was what might properly be called the Ferneydale Cézanne.

It was a self portrait. The painter, black-coated, black-bearded, was looking at you with black eyes from beneath the broad rim of a very black hat. To Gaston in his present circumstances there was something oppressive in the mere thought of what it would fetch in hard cash. Fulke's final venture in experimental psychology had after a malign fashion a touch of the princely about it. Gaston, however, was not prompted to behave with decent respect before this master-piece. He walked straight up to it, seized it by the frame, and then—instead of lifting it from the hook on which it might be judged to be suspended—rotated it through an angle of ninety degrees. As this was done in a clockwise direction Paul Cézanne tilted over back-wards, so that the hat might fairly have been expected to tumble from his head. The portrait now came away in Gaston's hands, to reveal a small and unpretending wall-cupboard on a simple latch. Gaston put the picture down, opened the cupboard, and withdrew the two photograph albums which it alone contained. His inspection of them was brief. As he had expected, there were no more Uffizi Venuses than when he had been shown the album by its owner several years before. But the Bronze Age striplings were considerably augmented. The final addition was indeed Bernie Huffer.

But now there was a more difficult search. The room abounded in typescript material. There were box files crammed with the stuff, and there were piles of it tied together with string. The first essential was to discover whether Bernie had imposed something like chronological order on the chaos. And there was immediate evidence that this was so. The spines of the box files had inscribed on them, in the same bold hand that had equated Gaston with Jesus Christ, *Bumf One, Bumf Two,* and so on into double figures. Gaston searched out the last of the series, opened it, and examined its contents. Here, sure enough, was the final discovery that was to be brought to Penelope's notice. It was a scenario-like performance of no more than three or four pages, but decidedly adequate to its purpose. Bernie had annotated it—lightly in pencil which could be readily rubbed out:

And here's the bloody damp squib.

Gaston felt that there were faint traces of a saving compunction distinguishable in Bernie. But this didn't mean that he ever wanted to run into him again. With the typescript in one hand and the photograph albums in the other, he went downstairs and returned to the living-room.

He needn't, he told himself, hurry about deciding what should be his next step. There was no reason to doubt Bernie's statement that Penelope meant not to return until the late afternoon, and it was now no more than lunch-time. He had better find himself something to eat, and when thus recruited think the matter out. But this reasonable plan he failed to put into immediate effect. The living-room was full of the warmth of the midday sun in June. It contained, however, a big fireplace for use in other seasons, and stacked beside this were several old newspapers and a bundle of faggots. Even in summer, he supposed, there might be chilly evenings from time to time. And what this sight told him was that he already knew what was the first thing to do.

Without difficulty he lit a fire, and when he had got a substantial blaze going he consigned to it those few pages of Fulke's typescript which outlined the story of a young Englishwoman who inherited a villa in France with disillusioning consequences. He then went to work on the photograph albums. The Venuses kindled at once; they curved, shrivelled, and were gone. The Bronze Age youths proved for some reason more resistant. Their extravagant pose, designed to express the dawning of intellect and awakening of *homo sapiens*, contorted itself further in the flames, so that they seemed to pass into nothingness, one by one, amid purgatorial fires. When the photographs were become grey ash Gaston, for good measure, fell to destroying the handsome leather albums in which they had been preserved. This was more difficult, and added to the effect of holocaust a grotesquely sacrificial smell. But they, too, became unrecognizable in the end. Then Gaston went into the kitchen and provided himself with a cheese sandwich and the better part of a bottle of wine. After that, he went outside and strolled up and down André's lawn. What he had done he by no means repented of. But there was still some stiff thinking ahead.

He had to admit that over an uncomfortably long period he had declined from the rôle of a patient and purposeful lover to that of a mere family friend of the Riches and Ferneydales alike. It had, indeed, been a rôle almost avuncular so far as Penelope was concerned. And now here he was in a very similar position at Le Colombier: an experienced older man, wise to the ways of the world, helping a young woman to escape the consequences of her own innocence of mind. That Penelope was not in fact an *ingénue*, and had indeed to be described as having her first youth a good way behind her, scarcely affected this. His unease, his sense of a trickiness in his situation, had, he supposed, something to do with the spirit of the age, which discounted the notion of there being any propriety in a quasi-paternal component in courtship and marriage. Few Emma Woodhouses were nowadays to be found wedded to Mr Knightleys.

But these were confused ideas, and his approaching crisis would be best met by not indulging them. He was convinced that he had done right in burning that bundle of rubbish, and he was equally clear that he must not prevaricate. The malignity of the whole design in which she was to have been involved must be explained to Penelope without evasions. And he mustn't regard his own effective intervention as any sort of passport to Penelope's affections. Or he must at least try not to do anything of the kind.

He returned to the house and prowled restlessly through it. The lavish nature of Fulke's munificence in its material regards again irked his mind and set it questioning. The Cézanne was the high-light here. With the money it would fetch you could buy a Le Colombier several times over. Add the Modigliani, the Giacometti, and sundry other *objets d'art* now for the first time coming within his notice, and the solid benefaction became very large indeed. How had Fulke viewed this? Penelope was to lose her head or her heart to Bernie Huffer, and was then to be humiliated by the conjoined discoveries of Bernie's true sexual disposition and her own rôle as a marionette in a minor Ferneydale literary project. And then, these revelations made, there Penelope was still to be: the sole possessor of a little private museum in the middle of France. Could Fulke have seen this as a large compensation for the small posthumous joke he had achieved? Gaston gave this charitable notion a fair scrutiny, and turned it down. Fulke Ferneydale, with all his skill as a writer, could sometimes be curiously in the dark about the anatomy of individual minds. But he could not conceivably believe that Penelope would continue to live on in the enjoyment of his villa.

With this thought in his mind, Gaston went into the open air again. He studied the view. He looked up at the sky. Two black kites were performing slow gyrations there, and his gaze lingered on them—reluctantly, as if they were creatures of ill omen. When he again looked down Penelope was standing before him.

'Charles,' Penelope said, 'how very nice! But however have you managed to turn up here?'

It was an awkward moment. 'However' was unavoidably 'why ever' as well, and the true answer had to be some politic modification of 'To meddle in your affairs'.

'I hired a car at Bordeaux,' Gaston said. 'It's a drive of only a few hours. And I can announce myself as your father's ambassador—although that's only a small part of the truth.'

'How very odd!' Penelope seemed amused rather than perplexed. 'But come into the house. Bernie Huffer will have spotted us, and be putting on the kettle. You mayn't have heard of Bernie. He was Fulke's secretary, and is still at Le Colombier, clearing things up.'

'I have heard of him. And in fact I've met him—here in your house earlier today. But clearing things up isn't his function. Messing things up would be nearer the mark. The truth is, Penelope, that I'm here to tell you something disagreeable about him.'

'Heavens above!' Penelope was looking at Gaston in an unnerving astonishment. 'You haven't come all the way from Mallows to tell me he's homosexual?'

It was some moments before Charles Gaston found a reply to this. To feel that he was in any sense making a fool of himself was to get off decidedly on the wrong foot.

'Well, that's the start of it,' he managed to say. 'And I suppose I needn't be surprised that you've become aware of the fact.'

'You can feel as surprised as you like. For what it's worth, I didn't become aware of it for quite some time. The penny only dropped with me a couple of days ago, when I'd properly interpreted something that occurred in the dovecot—which is where Bernie has his quarters here at Le Colombier. It somehow came together with some odd things I'd vaguely heard about Fulke long ago, and not much attended to. My walk this morning has been a kind of thinking walk, to decide whether there's anything I can do about it. It does seem such rotten luck, to be made that way.' For the first time, Penelope hesitated for a moment. 'But tumbling to the truth about Bernie did give me a very nasty jolt. I don't quite know why—except, I suppose, that I've grown rather fond of him. But I imagine there really isn't much one can do. Do you think, Charles, that any means can be found of helping him?'

Gaston's heart sank—or at least his mind misgave him—before such inferences as might have to be drawn from this unexpected attitude. Penelope, of course, was perfectly right in terms of her still only fragmentary knowledge of Bernie Huffer and what he had been lending himself to.

'There's quite a lot more to be told,' he said. 'And, for a start, I must tell you that Bernie isn't putting on that kettle. I asked him to pack up and go. And he went.'

'But, Charles, this is horrible! I can't think why you should presume to give such an order to Bernie, and still less can I understand why he obeyed you. I think it's wholly wrong: hounding people because their sexuality isn't quite like one's own.' Penelope was now very angry. 'And coming all the way from England to interfere in a perfectly gratuitous way! Do you take me for a child? And understand that, although I haven't known Bernie for long, I happen—as I've said—to like him a good deal.'

'Are you telling me, Penelope, that, having discovered about the young man's constitution, you've nevertheless decided to fall in love with him?'

'Charles, dear, you must be completely off your head—or think that I am.' Penelope had regained her composure, and showed no resentment in face of Gaston's bald question. In her glance at him, indeed, there might have been detected something like frank affection a little at odds with a most inappropriate glint of fun. 'I suppose, though, that it's a conceivable piece of nonsense for you to—well—get agitated about. Of course I've hated that miserable discovery. I'm prepared to say I've even been oddly wounded by it. But even before the truth came to me I couldn't have been in love with poor Bernie.' Penelope paused for a moment, almost as if seeking substantiating evidence for the truth of her assertion. 'Only consider, Charles! I'm old enough to be Bernie's mother.'

'You are nothing of the kind.'

'Well, certainly old enough to be his aunt.'

'Then you mean you've now come to feel a protective affection for him; that he has been revealed as a kind of endearing lame dog to be helped over his stile?'

'That expresses it not badly, I suppose.' Penelope seemed well content to settle promptly for this picture of things. 'Bernie is terribly vulnerable, you know. I see now that his perkiness—which I expect you met with—is an index of that. And I don't feel he really has much confidence in himself as a painter.'

'Listen, Penelope.' They had now crossed the lawn and entered the living-room. 'You are surprised that Bernie submitted to being turned out by me. Well, that's an index of something, too. We've got, so far, only to the fringes of the story.'

'The story?'

'One of Fulke's stories—devised by him, mounted regardless of expense, and with Bernie in an entirely wicked part that makes him something quite other than a lame dog. It may be hard for you to believe it without material evidence. And there *was* such evidence. Only I've destroyed it. Look over there.' Gaston pointed to the fireplace.

'Charles, whatever is all that mess?'

'A lot of mildly indecent photographs, which aren't very important except as a means of dismissing Bernie Huffer. But also the scenario for a revolting story, or perhaps one-act play.'

'But why ever have you burnt them?'

'I just thought them not fit for you to see. I suppose I have an old-fashioned mind. All the same, I mean to tell you the whole thing. And at once. Or as soon as you've made tea.'

*　　*　　*

204

They drove away together in Penelope's car on the following morning. For a time it was in silence, and then Penelope spoke.

'Charles, there's something I must say. You ought not to have had that cheerful little bonfire yesterday—if only because the things you destroyed were, after all, my property.'

'Good heavens, Penelope! You can't——'

'I don't mind about what you called the scenario. But didn't it occur to you that it might interest me to have a look at the little procession of Bernie's predecessors? All those golden boys.'

'Such an idea decidedly didn't come into my head.'

'Of course not. But I'm really trying to make a serious point. Women shouldn't be thought of as flapping around in search of protection. It's a bad basis for relationships.'

'Yes—only I didn't think of you as flapping around.'

'Dear Charles.' Penelope paused on this. 'I don't believe I'm ever going to like that house again.'

'Probably not. But I hope you won't see the drama we've wound up there as all tragedy.'

'It certainly hasn't occurred to me to view it as comedy.'

'I hope you'll come to do so. It has had its murky side, no doubt. But, Penelope, I'd like it to finish as comedies do.'

'With a happy ending?'

'Yes.'

For some minutes Penelope offered no rejoinder to this. When she did speak, it was to some effect of gaining further time.

'I suppose, Charles, that I can decently sell Le Colombier?'

'Certainly—and for a lot of money. But nothing like the money you'd get for its contents.'

'I'd not care for that at all. I'd feel like some virtuous heroine in Trollope who is rewarded with a huge fortune at the end of the story.'

'You can sell all, and give to the hungry. There are plenty of them round the globe. And that's what would suit my book.'

'Your book, Charles?'

'I'd feel less like that other sort of character in Trollope, who pursues a lady for her cash.'

'Oh, dear! Do you realize, Charles, that we've got ourselves into rather an awkward situation?'

'Isn't that precisely what we've got out of?'

'You know very well what I mean. You have put me under a great obligation to you. I've admitted I was getting fond of Bernie, although it wasn't—I'm quite sure it wasn't—in the way Fulke designed. But the end of Fulke's little fancy would have been very horrible, all the same. You're like a knight who has rescued a princess from the spell of the sorcerer.'

'I don't know that anything of that kind happens in Trollope.'

'It happens in romances of a different order. And the knight gets his princess as a matter of common form.'

'So he does.'

'But, Charles, we're not in that sort of story. So it's awkward. You once asked me to marry you, and I said I was never going to marry again. I believed it at the time, but it was a terribly rash thing to say.'

'Penelope——'

'So you see why it's awkward. You can't possibly ask me again now. There would be an unexpressed clause latent in your proposal. "Look what I've got you out of." Something like that. And don't tell me you haven't been seeing the difficulty.'

'I've been seeing nothing else since I came away from Mallows.'

'But there's a solution.' Penelope had slowed down the car rather abruptly—but perhaps only because ahead of them there was a cross-road without a *passage protégé*. 'It just entails my taking a small unfeminine initiative. Will you marry me?'

'Yes.'

'Then it's settled.' And Penelope, although now accelerating again, took a hand from the wheel and for certain moments laid it lightly on Charles Gaston's knee.